94/15

PEOPLE AND THEIR ENVIRONMENT

Series editor: Neil Punnett

Physical Environment and Human Activities

John Porter

NAME..

CLASS..

SUBJECT..

Oxford University Press

Oxford University Press, Walton St, Oxford
OX2 6DP

Oxford   New York   Toronto
Delhi   Bombay   Calcutta   Madras   Karachi
Petaling Jaya   Singapore   Hong Kong   Tokyo
Nairobi   Dar es Salaam   Cape Town
Melbourne   Auckland

and associated companies in
Berlin   Ibadan

Oxford is a trademark of Oxford University Press

© Oxford University Press 1989
First published 1989
Reprinted 1992

ISBN 0 19 913332 8

Typeset by Tradespools Ltd., Frome, Somerset
Printed in Hong Kong

Pupil Profile Sheets

A Pupil Profile base sheet is provided which can be copied to provide sheets for each pupil. It is intended that each pupil should receive a profile sheet at the end of each Study Unit in this book.

At the end of each Study Unit is an Assessment Unit. The second page of the Assessment Unit contains a box in which the details for the Pupil Profile Sheets are listed. The teacher can transfer the details to the base sheet.

The profile will be completed following discussion between the teacher and pupil. It will therefore provide an agreed record of achievement throughout the course. It is hoped that the profile will help to enhance the learning of pupils, increase motivation and provide diagnostic information for the teacher.

Acknowledgements

The publishers would like to thank the following for permission to reproduce photographs:

Aerofilms: p. 57, 92;   Agenzia ANSA: p. 23;   Bryan and Cherry Alexander: p. 65;   Art Directors Photo Library: p. 4 (top right); Aspect Picture Library: p. 4 (bottom), 51 (bottom), 74 (bottom), 88 (left), 103 (left) 121 (right);   K E Barber: p. 10 (top), 11;   Bettman Archive/Hulton Picture Company: p. 97;   Biofotos: p. 5, 7;   British Geological Survey/NERC: p. 70;   J. Allan Cash: p. 45;   Celtic Picture Agency:
p. 60, 68 (bottom);   John Cleare/Mountain Camera: p. 30, 49;   Derek Fordham/Arctic Camera: p. 59 (bottom);   Geoscience Features: p. 14 (bottom), 36 (top left, bottom left, bottom centre);   Richard and Sally Greenhill: p. 117 (left);   Susan Griggs: p. 26 (right), 28, 31 (top), 36 (top right, centre and bottom right), 112 (left), 114 (top), 117 (right); Hampshire County Council: p. 10 (bottom);   Robert Harding: p. 14 (top), 80 (top);   Jimmy Holmes/Himalayan Images: p. 9 (left); Keystone/Hulton Picture Company: p. 31 (left);   Frank Lane: p. 96; LKAB: p. 64;   Magnum: p. 98, 104, 122;   Marion and Tony Morrison: p. 102, 103 (right), 122 (left);   NASA: p. 4 (top left);   NRSC: p. 59 (top), 114 (centre);   Nigel Press Associates: p. 54 (bottom);   Norfolk Archeological Unit: p. 72, 111;   Oxford Scientific Films: p. 56 (left); Photo Library of Australia: p. 51 (top);   John Porter: p. 5 (top), 6, 46, 109;   Rapitest: p. 106;   Rex Features: p. 121 (left);   K E Sawyer: p. 74 (top);   Frank Spooner/Gamma: p. 101;   Solo Syndication: p. 39; Spectrum Colour Library: p. 86 (top), 88 (right), 119;   US Geological Survey: p. 77, 120;   University of Dundee: p. 80 (bottom);
A C Waltham: p. 9 (right), 26 (left), 48, 61, 69 (top);   Worldwide Fund for Nature: p. 112 (top), 115;   Geoffrey N. Wright: p. 63.

Contents

Unit 1: Natural environments

Our planet has been described as 'Spaceship Earth' (see Figure A). Do you think this is a good name for it? In what ways is the earth like a spaceship?

The planet earth is continually orbiting a much larger body in space, that is, the sun. The earth carries people, about 5000 million or so. By the twenty-second century this number will have doubled. The earth is self-supporting. Its only source of energy is the sun. The sun's energy is used directly and indirectly to support the environment we live in. It has often been argued that life exists on other planets, but it is unlikely. Only the earth's atmosphere seems to support life. All these features make the earth a unique 'spaceship'.

Our environment

Environment means 'surroundings' or the conditions which we find around us. We often use the term to mean our 'natural' surroundings. These include the biosphere, hydrosphere, and atmosphere.

● **The biosphere** is made up of animals, plants, and micro-organisms. It exists only on or very close to the surface of the earth. The interior of the earth is too hot to support life. High above the earth's surface the air is too thin and cold. Mankind is a major element of the biosphere.

● **The hydrosphere** consists of the oceans, seas, atmosphere, rivers, and lakes. It contributes to the feeding and maintenance of all life forms.

● **The atmosphere** encircles the biosphere and protects it from many of the harmful effects of the sun – for instance types of rays which harm body tissues. It shields the earth from bombardment by solid particles from space, and also helps to keep the earth's surface at a constant temperature.

The relief or shape of the land is another part of our natural environment.

Sometimes we also talk about the human or man-made environment, in

Figure A   A moon's-eye view of the earth

Figure B   Deer in a fragile oak-woodland environment

which we include buildings, industries, and cultivated land.

Unless you live in a very rural area, you will find that most of your environment is man-made. Although people are part of the biosphere, we have a far greater ability than other living creatures to adapt and modify our environment to our own needs. This makes it easy for us to believe that we don't need to depend on the natural environment any more.

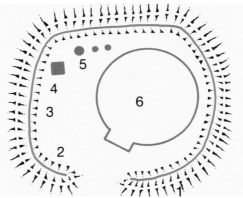

Figure D (*above*) Modern Reconstruction of an Iron Age farm at Butser Hill, Petersfield

Figure E (*left*) Plan of an Iron Age house:
1 ditch and bank
2 area for smelting iron
3 area for haystacks
4 cattle shelter
5 rubbish pits
6 house

Figure C Pollution and urban growth threaten the natural environment

QUESTIONS

1 Look out of your classroom window. Make a list of what you see and divide it into three sections headed:
   natural
   partly-natural (altered by man)
   man-made

2 Study the information in Figures D and E. They show what life might have been like about 2500 years ago in the Iron Age.
   a) Draw your own sketches of a modern home and farm.
   b) Look at all the figures on this page, and your own sketches. Which of the following statements do you think are true. Give reasons.
   i) We don't need the natural environment as much as we did.
   ii) We can change the natural environment to suit our needs.
   iii) Other people exploit the natural environment for us.
   iv) We are just as dependent as ever on the natural environment.
   v) We have forgotten how to use the natural environment.

Chain reaction in a pond

Figure A shows Fleet Pond in Hampshire. The pond is surrounded by beds of reeds growing on silt banks around the edges of the pond. The reed beds are gradually advancing towards the middle of the pond. As new reed beds are formed, the older ones gradually dry out and the saplings of trees such as oak, sweet chestnut, hazel, and birch grow on them. As Figure B shows, the pond is getting smaller gradually. It may soon disappear completely.

Why is this happening to Fleet Pond? Is there now more silt in the pond than there used to be? More silt around the pond edges means more banks for reeds to grow on. The silt is washed into the pond by streams. Figure B shows that there is quite a lot of reed growth close to where streams enter the pond, and around the edges where silt has been washed by currents.

We still need to know why there is so much silt being washed into the pond. One solution is that the soil in the surrounding area is being steadily eroded and washed into the streams. The land around the pond is owned by the army. Military training on this land may be churning up the ground so that the loose soil is easily washed away by the rain. Over the years the level of silt in the pond gradually builds up as a result of this chain of events.

This kind of chain reaction in the environment is called a *system*. In a system, *flows* or movements of energy or materials bring about changes. In the system we have just studied, movements of water and silt are helping to change the character of Fleet Pond.

Figure A Fleet Pond in Hampshire

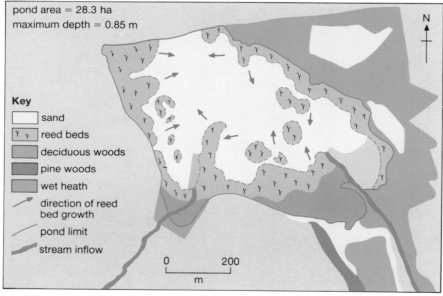

pond area = 28.3 ha
maximum depth = 0.85 m

Key
- sand
- reed beds
- deciduous woods
- pine woods
- wet heath
- direction of reed bed growth
- pond limit
- stream inflow

0   200
m

Figure B How Fleet Pond is gradually drying out

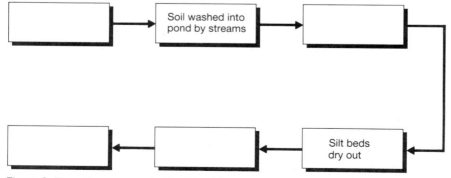

Soil washed into pond by streams

Silt beds dry out

Figure C The silting process in Fleet Pond (see question 1)

Features of systems

Your home also makes use of systems, for example, the electricity, water supply, and central heating systems. Think about what happens in a power cut. The electricity system stops working, and sometimes the central heating may go off as well. Even a gas-fired heating system will stop working in a power cut because there is no electricity to work the pump that circulates the hot water through the radiators!

Figure D shows the main systems that bring about changes in the environment. These systems operate in a circular or *cyclical* way and are powered by the sun's energy. They are:

● the *water cycle*, which involves the circulation of water in different forms through the atmosphere, rivers, and seas.

● the *biocycle*, which is made up of *ecosystems* in which life-forms are created, decay, and become the nutrients of new life forms.

● the *rock cycle*, which involves the wearing down of material from the earth's surface and its use in making new rock materials in many millions of years time.

Figure D shows that these systems are not only linked together, but that mankind forms an essential part of them. People have stepped into many environmental systems and altered them to serve their own needs. For instance a farmer is using nature's capacity to grow plants and breed animals to serve his own commercial purposes. Environmental systems can, of course, work the other way round, producing hazards which limit people's activities. Can you think of examples of this? We will be looking at many further on in this book.

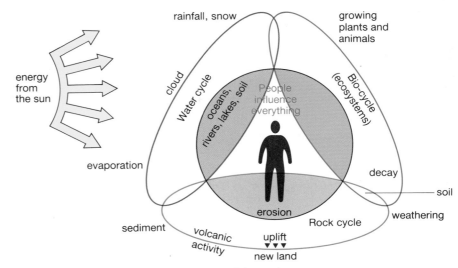

Figure D The main environmental systems of the earth

QUESTIONS

1 Study Figures A and B:

a) How big is this pond? How deep is it?

b) What sort of soil is there around the pond?

c) How does your answer to b) help to explain why there is so much silt in the pond?

d) Which parts of the pond are becoming most overgrown with reeds?

e) The following is a list of the changes which are affecting the pond. Rearrange them in the order they happen:

    silt washed by streams into pond
    trees take over from reeds
    army exercises loosen soil
    silt beds build up
    silt beds dry out
    soil washed by rain into streams
    reeds grow on silt beds

f) Use the list from e) to complete the *flow diagram* (Figure C). This is a series of boxes linked by arrows. It shows you the order in which changes happen, and how changes in one part of the system bring about changes in others. Give your diagram a suitable title.

2 Study the diagram of environmental systems (Figure D) and then look at the picture of a Scottish glen (Figure E). What evidence can you find in the photograph of:

    the water cycle?
    the biocycle?
    the rock cycle?

3 Look again at the Iron Age study on page 5. Which environmental systems was man beginning to make use of in the Iron Age?

4 One way of understanding a system better is to set up an idea or 'hypothesis' about it and test it out. For instance:

'There are more reed beds near stream outlets into my local lake or pond than elsewhere in the pond.'

What information would you need to collect to 'test out' this hypothesis?

Figure E Glen Docherty stream (see question 2)

1.3 Environmental hazards

In earlier times people's lives were much more closely linked to their natural environment than they are today. This was especially true when most families used the land to produce their own food. Urbanisation has made many people much less directly dependent on their natural surroundings. In the United Kingdom, we may complain sometimes about the weather, but there are few other natural or environmental controls which directly worry us all that much.

Figure A Location of the Karakoram Mountains

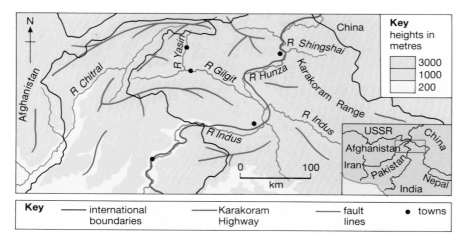

Key
— international boundaries
— Karakoram Highway
— fault lines
• towns

Figure B Natural hazards in order of priority as seen by the people of the Karakoram Mountains

Natural hazards	Impact on the local community	Ways to reduce or remove the risks	
		Possible solutions	Major difficulties
Failure of water supply	Loss or damage to crops and animals and farming land	Relocate settlements on better sites	High cost
Land erosion	Damage to buildings		Lack of expertise
Flooding	Risk to health from drinking contaminated river water	Flood control measures (banks, ditches, dams) and warning systems	Few alternative sites
Earthquakes, which cause landslides and rockfalls	General hardship		Social upheaval
	May result in abandonment of settlements	Education	Unwillingness to move or change way of life and building methods
Earthquakes	Loss of human life	New and safe construction methods	

The Karakoram

In other parts of the world the environment is much more hazardous for people. The area in Figure A shows the Karakoram Mountains of Northern India and North-east Pakistan. Here people have to face a wide range of environmental hazards. The region is in one of the world's major earthquake belts (see page 13). Since 1900, over 1250 000 people have died in earthquakes in the Karakoram. A single earthquake in 1976 killed 242 000 people.

Earthquakes in the Karakoram bring with them other natural hazards. They cause landslides and rockfalls, which besides damaging villages and houses, can ruin cultivation terraces on the hillsides. By blocking river channels, landslides may cause widespread flooding and disrupt water supplies. Floods wash away valuable topsoil from the hillsides. Figure B summarises these hazards and their effects.

Deaths from earthquakes and other hazards in the Karakoram have been high partly because of the way local people build their houses (Figure D). Buildings have thick walls of stone and timber beams, and heavy timbers are used for the roofs. Because these walls have no proper framing or structure they easily collapse when they are shaken by an earth tremor.

Figure C Hazard flow diagram (see question 3)

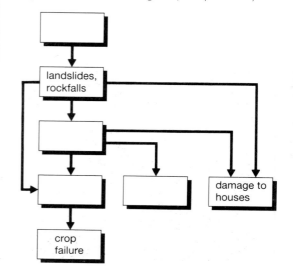

Living with hazards

A scientific survey team studied the area and found that the only way to remove the risks altogether would be to relocate villages. But there were few alternative sites. A move from hillside to valley would lessen the danger of landslides, but increase the risk of flash flooding. Villagers were not keen to move in any case. They did not want to leave their traditional homes, crops and livelihoods.

Figure B lists ways the survey team thought that the impact of hazards could be reduced. With all these solutions however there were problems of cost and technical knowledge. In the Karakoram there is little opportunity for villagers to receive the technical education they would need to build better quality houses or protective walls, or dig bigger river channels to take flood waters. In any case the costs are well beyond what they can afford, and they need all their time to grow the crops required for survival.

In the Karakoram, people are prepared to overlook the hazards of their natural surroundings so that they can deal with their everyday problems. Perhaps this explains why many people live in hazardous areas of the world despite the risks involved. On page 120 you will read about Los Angeles, one of the world's largest and wealthiest cities. A major disaster is expected at any time, but people go on living there anyway.

Figure E Settlements overshadowed by the Karakoram range. People who live in this region care more about things like schooling, health care and their crops than they do about natural hazards

Figure D Buildings typical of the Karakoram area

QUESTIONS

1 With the help of an atlas:
   a) Name *two* countries outside India and Pakistan which lie close to the Karakoram Mountains.
   b) Name the larger range of mountains of which the Karakoram is a part.
   c) What is the average height of mountains in the Karakoram?
   d) Try to find some reasons why the Karakoram area is vulnerable to earthquakes (see pages 12–17).

2 **a)** Describe how houses in the Karakoram are constructed.
   b) Explain why such houses are often unable to withstand the shock of earthquakes or landslides.

3 Copy and complete Figure C with the help of the list below:

   earthquakes   failure of water supply
   flooding   land and soil erosion

4 Below is a list of some of the problems of living experienced by Karakoram people. Put the list in rank order of importance, as it might be ranked by a Karakoram villager. Justify the highest and lowest rankings on your list.

   crop prices   lack of medicine   floods
   no schools   rockfalls   crop failure
   lack of firewood

5 What other problems could be added to the list in question **4**?

6 Write the section of the survey team's report headed **What is needed**. In it outline some proposals for schemes which might make life easier for Karakoram people. Justify your proposals, but also point out the problems they involve.

Figure A Students walking towards Cranes Moor in the New Forest

Figure B Traffic congestion in Lyndhurst in summer

Figure C Location map of the New Forest

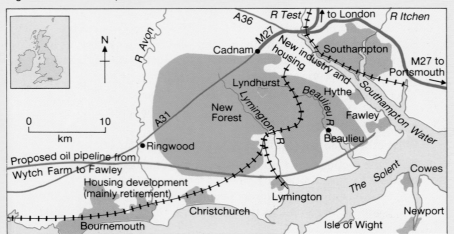

The New Forest

The New Forest is the largest area of uncultivated vegetation in England and one of the largest in Europe. It contains many habitats of wildlife that have become rare elsewhere in Britain. Old forest court rolls maintain the rights of commoners (people living in the Forest) to pasture animals. The New Forest has become increasingly popular with tourists, particularly motorists and campers.

1   Study the photographs of different parts of the New Forest:
   a) Describe the landscape in Figure A   (3 marks)
   b) Name *two* things people come to do in the New Forest   (2 marks)

2   Look at the forest facts panel below. What facts provide more detailed information about what there is in the pictures?   (5 marks)

3   You need to be sure that you know the locations of all the places you study. Use the map (Figure C) to describe the location of the New Forest in relation to:
   a) nearby towns   (2 marks)
   b) nearby cities   (2 marks)
   c) motorways   (2 marks)
   d) coastal features   (2 marks)

4   Figure F shows how the number of campers has increased since 1955. Present the same data as a:
   a) table   (5 marks)
   b) line graph   (5 marks)

```
FOREST FACTS
Area   375 sq km
Heathland and grassland   11740 ha
Valley marshes   238 ha
Open deciduous woodland   4049 ha

Owner   Ministry of Agriculture
Administered by   Forestry Commission

Number of commoners   300–400
Number of cattle and ponies   over 5000
Number of visitors   8–10 million per year
```

5 You will find many sections of this book that deal with environmental issues. Study the panel below which relates to the conservation aims and problems in the New Forest. Answer the questions below:

a) How does human activity cause problems to the environment of the New Forest   (4 marks)

b) What has been done to overcome these problems?
      (4 marks)

6 From what you have studied do you think that the New Forest environment is under threat? Give reasons for your answer.   (4 marks)

Total: 40 marks

Aims of the 1971–79 conservation plan

- to restrict camping to twelve main sites
- to prohibit cars from minor roads
- to create many new small car parks and picnic sites
- to create forest walks to provide people with enjoyment but to keep them away from sensitive areas

Problems that remain

- need for easier access for day visitors to the M27 motorway
- new housing developments close to the Forest
- oil pipeline routes through the Forest
- changes to vegetation if the numbers of commoners drop and fewer ponies and cattle are grazed

---

Figure D A camp site among the trees

Details of pupil profile sheet Unit 1

Knowledge and understanding

1 The earth is a self-supporting body receiving all its energy from the sun
2 The sun powers the earth's natural systems or cycles
3 Human activities can change the working of natural systems
4 Natural hazards can influence patterns of human activity

Skills

1 Observation of natural and man-made features
2 Completion of flow diagram from data
3 Setting up and testing hypothesis
4 Use of atlas
5 Basic skills used in geographical studies

Values

1 Awareness of our continuing dependence on the natural environment
2 Awareness of how people perceive natural hazards

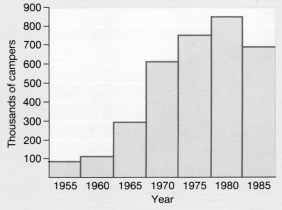

Figure E Growth in the number of campers in the New Forest

Unit 2: Building the landscape

The earth's surface is moving constantly under your feet. The continents are gradually shifting in position. Trace maps of South America and Africa from the atlas. Cut out the outlines. Notice how well the west coast of Africa fits into the eastern coast of South America. Geologists, who study the earth and its rocks, believe that all the continents once formed one huge land mass. The process by which the continents have broken apart is called *continental drift*.

Plate tectonics

About twenty years ago a geologist put forward a theory called *plate tectonics* (Figure B). The main ideas behind this theory were:

● The earth's crust is divided into a number of rigid blocks called *plates* (see Figure C).

● *Continental plates* contain pieces of ocean floor as well as pieces of continents. *Oceanic plates* form only ocean floors.

● Oceanic crust is denser and heavier than continental crust.

● The plates are constantly moving – towards, away from, or against each other along *plate boundaries* (see Figure B).

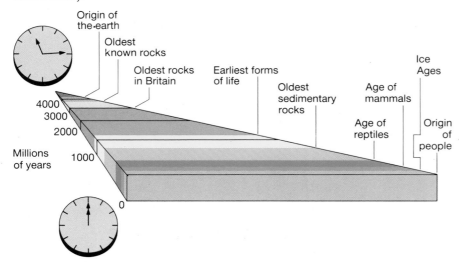

Figure A An imaginary time-table for the major events in the earth's history.

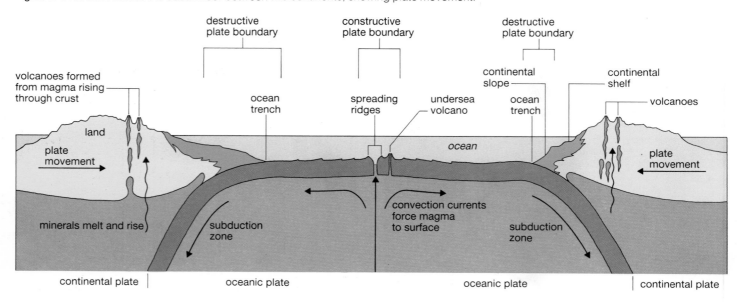

Figure B A section across the ocean floor between two continents, showing plate movement.

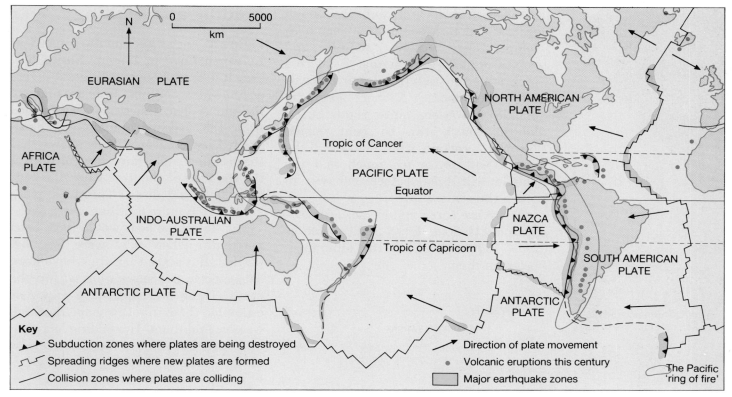

Figure C Plate boundaries, earthquake zones and volcanoes. Notice how close all the volcanoes are to the plate boundaries.

Crustal shocks and fractures

Plate movement causes a great deal of stress and tension, particularly along plate boundaries. As the plates pull away from each other along the *spreading ridges*, huge cracks or faults called *transform faults* develop (Figure C). Along *collision* and *subduction* zones, stress and strain lead to violent shocks or tremors. We call these *earthquakes*. Along many boundaries, cracks in the crust form points of weakness. Along these fractures hot magma under pressure forces its way to the surface. This makes many plate boundaries sources of *volcanic activity*.

QUESTIONS

1 From the text and Figure B find terms to describe:
  a) cracks in the earth's crust
  b) continents pulling apart
  c) the edge of a continent

2 a) Decide which of the following statements are true or false.
    i) The continents have always been fixed in position.
    ii) Earthquakes are a result of plate movement.
    iii) Most spreading ridges are under the sea.
    iv) Plate tectonics is a very old theory.
  b) Correct the false statements.

3 The time is 12 midnight. Imagine that the earth began to exist only 46 minutes ago, at 11-14 p.m.
  a) With the help of Figure A, complete the time-table below:

    11-15 p.m.   Earth formed from Solar System
    11-30 p.m.   Oldest known rocks in Britain formed
    11-50 p.m.   ...

  b) From your time-table how long has mankind been on the earth?

3 Practical exercise
  a) On an outline map of the world, mark the plate boundaries.
  b) Obtain a list of the world's biggest cities and their populations. Show the position of these cities on your map.
  c) How many cities lie on or close to plate boundaries? How many people live in these cities? How many people is this altogether?
  d) Write about the different ways in which people living in urban areas close to plate boundaries may be at risk.

13

2.2 Rocks: stress and tension

'Solid as a rock' is a common enough saying. But rock heated to a very high temperature becomes molten, and moves or flows like liquid. Even cold rock is not entirely solid, but behaves more like plastic. A short length of plastic will seem quite rigid, but a longer length can be bent easily. Beyond a certain point, however, the strain will prove too much and the plastic will break. Rock behaves in much the same way.

There are three main types of rock — *igneous*, *sedimentary*, and *metamorphic*. Figure A shows the differences between them.

Folding and faulting

Figure B shows sedimentary rocks at Lulworth Cove in Dorset. Notice how easy it is to pick out the different layers or *beds*. Many of these beds are made of limestone. The limestone was formed from the crushed remains of hard-shelled sea creatures. This shows that the location must have formed part of the sea floor at the time when the beds were first laid down. This took place about two hundred million years ago.

The limestone beds would have been horizontal when they were first deposited. But since then they have been subjected to pressures from within the earth. These pressures have *folded* or crumpled them into the shape in which we now find them. The folding has been so severe that some of the beds are now almost vertical. The fold is known locally as the 'Lulworth Crumple'.

A geologist looking at the rocks in Figure C would know that he was look-

Figure A The main types of rock and how they are formed

Sedimentary rocks

- Formed from deposits of old rock material, animal shells, or plant remains
- Deposited in layers, often the sea bed
- Contain fossils
- Often found deformed (folded or crumpled)
- Usually softer than igneous rocks, more easily worn away
- Examples: sandstone, limestone and chalk

Volcanic rocks

Weathering and erosion

Transport by wind and water

Sedimentary rocks

Deposition

Metamorphic rocks

Sedimentary rocks

Intrusive igneous rocks

Magma reservoir

Igeneous rocks

- Formed by the cooling of molten magma
- Volcanic rocks are formed from solidified lava
- Easily recognised by crystals
- Not easily worn away by the weather
- Examples: granite (large crystals), basalt (small crystals), obsidian (volcanic)

Metamorphic rocks

- Formed from other rocks under great heat and pressure
- Contain new minerals formed out of original ones
- Original layering usually destroyed
- Examples: slate (from shale), marble (from limestone)

Figure B The Lulworth Crumple, showing folded sedimentary rocks

Figure C Faults in rock beds. Notice how the layers of rock are displaced

Figure D (*right*) Some structures found in rocks

Anticline or upfold

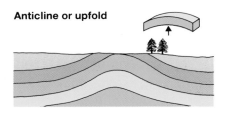

Syncline or downfold

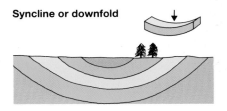

ing at *faults*. These are fractures in the rock structure caused by strain or *tension*. Figure D shows the different types of folds and faults. Study them carefully.

Rocks and people

Rocks are an important economic resource (see Figure E). Some rocks are valuable for the minerals they contain while others are quarried for building materials and making chemicals.

The structure of rocks influences how easy or difficult it is for people to use them. Rocks close to the surface are easier and cheaper to work than those at depth. Rocks with many faults or folds are very difficult to mine or quarry. They may be so expensive to work that it is not worth the trouble.

Thrust fault
Fold has fractured

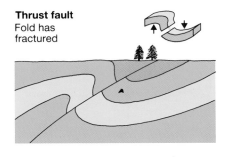

Normal fault
Rocks have fractured and stretched

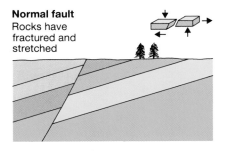

Reverse fault
Rocks have fractured and been pushed together

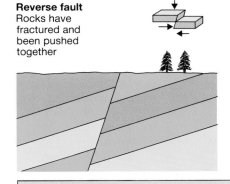

Rift valley
Ground sinks between two faults

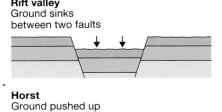

Horst
Ground pushed up between two faults

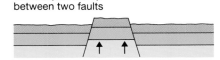

Figure E The main uses of some common rocks

Type of rock	Everyday use
Granite	Building materials, gravestones, road chippings
Slate	Roofing material, paving tiles
Limestone	Building stone, dry stone walls, cement
Chalk	Cement
Sandstone	Building stone, pavements
Clay	Brick and tile making
Coal	Fuel
Gravel	Concrete making

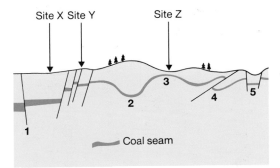

Figure F Cross-section of a coal seam (see question 2)

QUESTIONS

1 Use the text and diagrams to help you name a rock which:
   a) has large crystals
   b) was formed from the remains of hard-shelled sea creatures
   c) is used as a roofing material
   d) was laid down in beds
   e) is not easily worn down by the weather

2 Figure F is a cross-section through rocks that contain a coal seam. The coal seam is shown in red.
   a) How is coal formed?
   b) Name the features shown by the numbers **1–5**
   c) British Coal is considering developing a new coal mine at one of the three locations **X**, **Y**, or **Z** shown on the section. Copy and complete the table below:

Benefits and problems of proposed sites for new coal mine

Factor	Site X	Site Y	Site Z
Depth of seam Problems of working Thickness of seam			

   d) Write a report based on the completed table and Figure F. Mention other factors British Coal might have to take account of before the company can take a decision.

2.3 Earthquakes: Armenia, Japan and California

The newspaper extract (Figure A) is about an earthquake which took place in Armenia in 1988. Armenia is in the south-west of the USSR, near the border with Turkey. Earthquakes are often reported in detail in newspapers because they usually occur very suddenly and cause a lot of damage and injury. Figure B shows some features of earthquakes and how they are measured.

The Armenian earthquake started with a build-up of stress in rocks lying against each other along a fault. The stress resulted from pressures within the crust. The shock occurred as the rocks 'jumped back' against each other in order to relieve the stress. The sudden movement caused energy to travel outwards in waves, bringing about the total destruction of buildings on the surface above.

Measuring and locating earthquakes

The strength of earthquake waves is measured on a seismograph. Look at the seismograph 'trace' in Figure B. The trace is made as a pen moves over a sheet of paper which is attached to a slowly rotating drum. Earthquake waves cause the pen to vibrate and mark out long sweeps on the paper. Notice how the seismograph has recorded three sets of waves. This record can be used to work out how far away from the seismograph the shock occurred. The records of any three seismographs can then be used to fix the position of the epicentre. Question 2 gives you a chance to do this.

Earthquake devastates Armenia

Mr Gorbachev, the Soviet leader, arrives in Armenia this morning to take charge of relief operations after Wednesday's earthquake. Mr Gorbachev cut short his visit to the United States and headed for Yerevan, the Armenian capital. 'I have to be there in this effort', he said.

When the dust settles, it is expected that the earthquake will be the worst ever in the Soviet Union. No specific casualty figures were available, but Soviet officials spoke of tens of thousands dead.

The earthquake, which also affected parts of Turkey, Iran, and the neighbouring Soviet republic of Georgia, registered nine points on the Mercalli scale. Its epicentre was near Leninakan, a city of 200 000 people near the Turkish border. Reports said that three quarters of the city had been destroyed. Tremors continued last night with many people afraid to return to their homes.

Two army sergeants helping in the emergency spoke of pulling the bodies of more than 50 children from the ruins of a collapsed primary school in Leninakan. The nearby town of Spitak, with a population of 16 000, was hardest hit. Only one of eight schools were said to be still standing. Blood was being collected nationwide and tons of relief supplies were being airlifted into the region.

Figure A A Newspaper report of the Armenian earthquake

Figure B Earthquake features (**a**, **b**), seismograph trace (**c**), rate of travel of L, S and P waves (**d**), Richter scale (**e**), Mercalli scale (**f**)

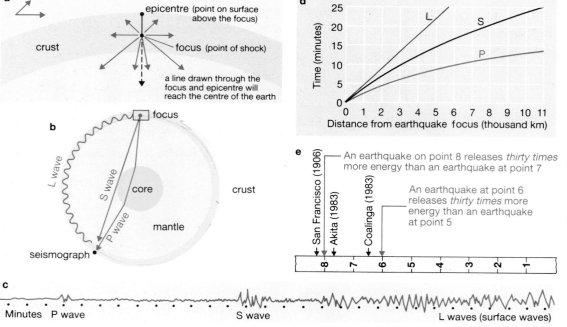

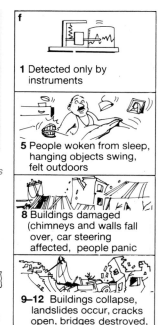

Colliding plates

Armenia is on one of the world's major collision zones. Along this zone the southward-moving Eurasian plate is colliding with the Turkish plate. The collision is part of a pattern of plate movements which produced the fold mountains of the Himalayas millions of years ago.

A geologist explained why it was not easy to predict the earthquake. 'In some places there is continuous small activity, which means that all the stress is released gently. When nothing happens for a long while, you know the stress is building up, but you don't know when it will be released. While you are trying to predict the earthquake, it just sneaks up behind you and hits you.'

Earthquakes and tsunamis

Coastal regions are especially at risk from earthquake damage. Where an earthquake occurs offshore it may generate a *tsunami* or 'tidal' wave. When a tsunami strikes the shoreline the damage can be catastrophic. In 1983 an earthquake of Richter force 7.7 produced a tsunami off the coast of northwest Japan near Akita (see Figure E). Ten-foot high waves swept 70 people out to sea, leaving 30 dead. Fishing boats were upturned and wrecked cars floated in the sea after being sucked out by the receding water.

Figure D The Akita tsunami of 1983: the crane was demolished seconds later

The San Andreas fault

A huge earthquake hit the city of San Francisco in 1906. It was caused by rocks along the San Andreas fault moving sideways against each other by up to six metres. The earthquake was of magnitude 8.3 on the Richter scale and severe shaking lasted for a minute. Seven hundred people died and there was widespread destruction of buildings. Much of the damage was caused by fires that broke out after the shock.

Since 1906 new buildings in San Francisco have been designed to withstand possible future earthquakes. Even so, seismologists think that if another earthquake occurs the damage may be just as devastating as it was in 1906. Buildings constructed on soft ground rather than on solid rock will be particularly at risk. Elevated motorways will be destroyed and glass falling from high-rise buildings is expected to cause a lot of injury.

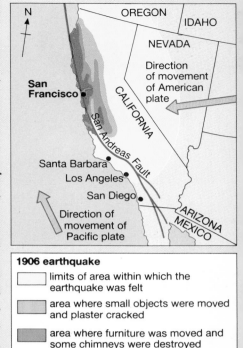

1906 earthquake

- limits of area within which the earthquake was felt
- area where small objects were moved and plaster cracked
- area where furniture was moved and some chimneys were destroyed
- area of structural damage to buildings

Figure C The San Andreas fault,

QUESTIONS

1 a) Why were so many more lives lost in the Armenian earthquake than in the Akita one?

b) Why was it not possible to predict the Armenian earthquake?

2 a) On the sample seismograph trace in Figure B measure the time gap between the arrival of P and S waves.

b) Make a copy of the graph in Figure B. On your copy draw a series of vertical lines about a centimetre apart.

c) Use your vertical lines to help you to work out the distance of the seismograph from the earthquake focus.

d) The figure below shows the location of three seismographs. Each seismograph recorded an equal time gap between the arrival of P and S waves. The time gap is as calculated by you above. Trace this map. Now use a pair of compasses to draw circles to locate the epicentre of the earthquake.

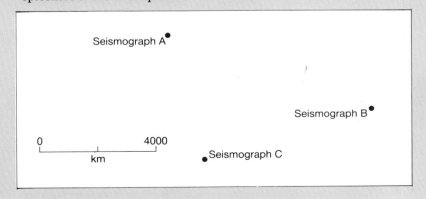

2.4 Mount St Helens 1: The eruption

Figure A (*right*) Mount St Helens erupting on 18 May 1980

Figure B (*below*) How the eruption happened

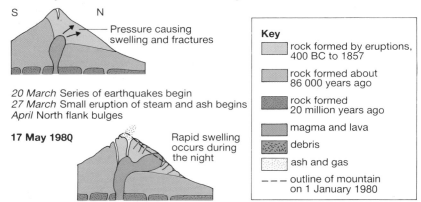

1 January 1980 Mount St Helens is 2950 m high and covered in ice and snow

S   N

— Pressure causing swelling and fractures

20 March Series of earthquakes begin
27 March Small eruption of steam and ash begins
April North flank bulges

17 May 1980

Rapid swelling occurs during the night

Key

	rock formed by eruptions, 400 BC to 1857
	rock formed about 86 000 years ago
	rock formed 20 million years ago
	magma and lava
	debris
	ash and gas
– – –	outline of mountain on 1 January 1980

18 May 1980 *8.00 am* Earthquake triggers huge landslide of rock, glacier ice and soil
8.32 am Mountainside collapses

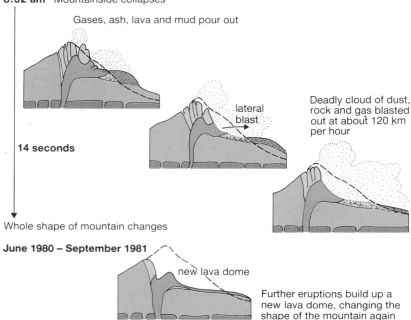

Gases, ash, lava and mud pour out

lateral blast

Deadly cloud of dust, rock and gas blasted out at about 120 km per hour

14 seconds

Whole shape of mountain changes

June 1980 – September 1981

new lava dome

Further eruptions build up a new lava dome, changing the shape of the mountain again

At 8.32 am on 18 May 1980 an earthquake triggered the collapse of the north side of Mount St Helens (Figure A), in the state of Washington, USA. Mount St Helens is a volcano which had not been *active* since 1857. Its eruption was the first volcanic event in the USA since 1917. Not surprisingly the eruption attracted a lot of public and scientific interest. Scientists had been predicting the eruption and were prepared to follow its progress second by second. Even so, the fury of the eruption took the scientists by surprise and several of them were killed.

How the eruption happened

Figure B shows the chain of events from 1 January to September 1981. Mount St Helens steamed and smoked, bulged and then blew up. In 14 seconds a deadly cloud of hot ash, dust, rocks and gas, travelling at 120 km per hour, destroyed huge areas of forest, wiped out wildlife, and killed 60 people. The shape of the mountain changed completely.

What caused the eruption?

Mount St Helens is one of many volcanic peaks in the Cascade Range of Washington and Oregon states. The peaks have been built up by a series of eruptions over the last 20 million years. On the map (Figure C) note how the small Juan de Fuca plate is moving away from the Pacific plate. The Juan de Fuca plate is being pushed under the North American plate and is forming a deep oceanic trench.

The Juan de Fuca plate is being pushed downwards at about 2 cm every year. As it descends it melts because of the high temperatures deep in the earth's crust. Here it forms molten rock or *magma* (see Figure B on page 12). This magma is less dense than the rocks surrounding it, and so it tends to rise back towards the surface, a distance of about 100 km. It may become trapped just below solid surface rock where it forms magma reservoirs. The magma is often under pressure. Where earthquakes cause fractures in the surrounding rocks, through which pressure can be released, an eruption is almost certain to occur.

These conditions threaten the whole of the Cascade Range of mountains with eruptions triggered off by earthquakes.

Types of volcanoes

As Figure D shows, volcanoes are classified according to certain qualities. These are:

● shape
● how they are formed
● what they are made of

Some volcanoes are erupting all the time. The eruptions are gentle and at regular time intervals, like a hiccup releasing the pressure underneath. In other cases the pressure builds up over a long period, and when the volcano finally blows its top it does so with devastating effect. In the case of Mount St Helens the eruption had been predicted, and most people had been evacuated by the time it took place.

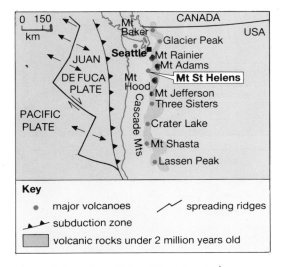

Figure C Location of Mount St Helens in the Cascade mountains

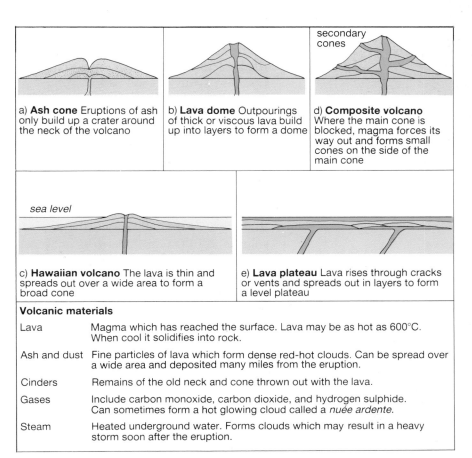

a) **Ash cone** Eruptions of ash only build up a crater around the neck of the volcano

b) **Lava dome** Outpourings of thick or viscous lava build up into layers to form a dome

d) **Composite volcano** Where the main cone is blocked, magma forces its way out and forms small cones on the side of the main cone

c) **Hawaiian volcano** The lava is thin and spreads out over a wide area to form a broad cone

e) **Lava plateau** Lava rises through cracks or vents and spreads out in layers to form a level plateau

Volcanic materials

Lava	Magma which has reached the surface. Lava may be as hot as 600°C. When cool it solidifies into rock.
Ash and dust	Fine particles of lava which form dense red-hot clouds. Can be spread over a wide area and deposited many miles from the eruption.
Cinders	Remains of the old neck and cone thrown out with the lava.
Gases	Include carbon monoxide, carbon dioxide, and hydrogen sulphide. Can sometimes form a hot glowing cloud called a *nuée ardente*.
Steam	Heated underground water. Forms clouds which may result in a heavy storm soon after the eruption.

Figure D Composition and types of volcanoes

QUESTIONS

1 Study Figure C:
   a) In which range of mountains is Mount St Helens?
   b) Name *three* other volcanic peaks which are within 200 km of this mountain.

2 Produce a time-table for the eruption of Mount St Helens, using the following headings: *Date, Time, Event*.

3 Name and describe *three* materials which the Mount St Helens eruption produced.

4 Explain the role of the following in the Mount St Helens eruption:
   a) plate movement   d) earthquakes
   b) subduction   e) fractures
   c) density of magma

5 Do any of the types of volcanic forms listed in Figure D describe Mount St Helens?

6 'Will St Helens continue to build until it surpasses its former majesty, or will it blow itself apart in a new fury of destruction?'
   (*National Geographic Magazine*, 1981)
   Which possibility do you think seems the most likely to occur during the next few years? Justify your view.

2.5 Mount St Helens 2: After the eruption

The effects of 18 May 1980 were not limited to the scene of the eruption itself. The eruption changed the environment over a wide area (Figure A) and affected the lives of many people.

Rivers

When the mountain erupted, the sides of the volcano were still covered with ice and snow from the winter. The intense heat melted the ice and snow to release 200 000 million litres of water. The water turned the debris from the landslide into huge mudflows which poured into the river valleys and blocked them.

The North Toutle River was one of the worst hit. The valley floor was raised by up to 200 metres. With its natural channel clogged, the river began to wander freely over the debris surface. It cut away embankments and began to form new meanders which threatened bridges, roads, and railways. At one vital bridge the American army spent 18 months digging away 100 million cubic metres of debris. By doing this they rechannelled the river and prevented further flooding.

Coldwater Lake, a reservoir in the catchment area of the North Toutle, became so full that it threatened to break its dam. To lower the lake to a safe level a new 1000 metre-long exit channel had to be dug during the weeks after the eruption.

Debris reduced the flow of the River Columbia so much that ships were trapped in the harbour at Portland. Intensive dredging was needed before the port could be reopened.

Figure A The effects of the Mount St Helens eruption

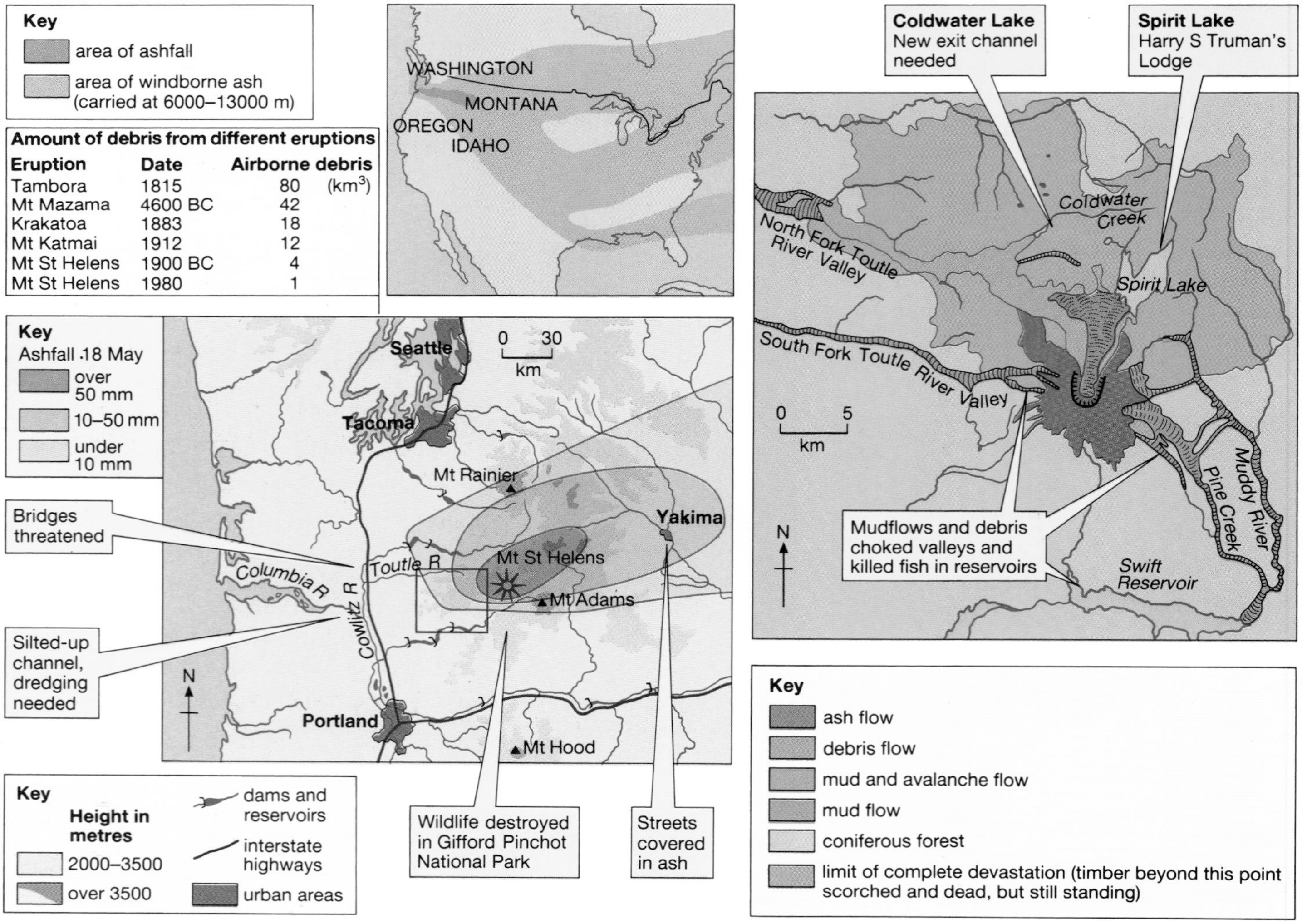

Amount of debris from different eruptions

Eruption	Date	Airborne debris (km^3)
Tambora	1815	80
Mt Mazama	4600 BC	42
Krakatoa	1883	18
Mt Katmai	1912	12
Mt St Helens	1900 BC	4
Mt St Helens	1980	1

Wildlife and forests

The hot mud pouring into rivers raised the temperature of the water to 30° C, killing most forms of water life and destroying fish eggs. Small creatures choked to death on the gas and ash. Hundreds of elk, bears, cougars, and mountain goats in the Gifford Pinchot National Park were destroyed. Altogether two million fish, birds, and animals perished in the explosion. Although some forms of insect life – such as flies and ants – began to revive quickly, scientists estimate that it may take forty years for the wildlife of the area to get back to normal.

The sides of Mount St Helens had been covered with pine, spruce, fir, and hemlock forests. The blast destroyed these forests, creating huge areas of scorched logs which rolled down the valley sides and blocked rivers. Timber companies managed to salvage some of this timber. It was estimated that ten million new seedlings will be needed to restore the area's forests.

The atmosphere

A huge cloud of ash was carried eastwards by prevailing winds. Most of it fell in Washington and western Montana where some places had 70 mm of ashfall. The ash cloud steadily widened as it drifted east and was seen over much of the United States (Figure A). Within 17 days it had circled the globe.

Scientists thought that the eruption might lead to colder climates by the dust absorbing incoming solar radiation. Although the eruption was spectacular it produced much less dust than some other recent volcanic eruptions. There was little effect on global climate.

People

Mount St Helens is a favourite area for camping, backpacking, and fishing. It also has various logging camps for the timber industry. Fortunately, since the eruption had been expected, most people were evacuated from the danger area. Nevertheless sixty people were killed.

Throughout Washington, Montana, and Idaho transport was disrupted: cars stalled, electricity supplies were cut, and food supplies were threatened. Public access to the region was severely limited because of the fears of further eruptions.

QUESTIONS

1 Study Figure A:
  a) Name *three* places affected by the eruption. In each case state how each place was affected.
  b) Copy the main features of the right-hand map. On your copy draw a circle with a radius of 20 km with Mount St Helens in the middle. Colour it in. List the main effects of the eruption within this area.

2 **a)** Produce a checklist of as many effects as you can find in the text and pictures. Your list might start off like this:
      blocked valleys
      embankments cut
      bridges threatened
  b) Now draw up a table with the three headings shown below and copy your list of effects into the appropriate columns.

Immediate effects (dealt with in a few days)	Short-term effects (dealt with over several months)	Long-term effects (dealt with only over several years)

  c) Write a paragraph about how long the effects of the eruption lasted.

3 The viewpoints of four people about the eruption are shown below. Select *one* person's opinion and say how it compares with the other three.

"I need to get just one more sequence of pictures."

ROBERT LANDSBURG, photographer who never returned from the mountain

"I talk to the mountain, the mountain talks to me, I am part of that mountain, the mountain is part of me."

HARRY S. TRUMAN, elderly resident of the mountain, refused to leave and died during the eruption

"Yuck! Three feet of mud all over the place."

JOE HALLECK, schoolboy from Toutle

"It's been costing us 100,000 dollars a day. Yakima doesn't have the resources. The state and federal governments must help."

LARRY WITTENBERG, official of town of Yakima

2.6 Pozzuoli: town on a volcano

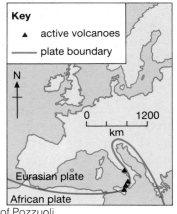

Figure A (*right*) The location of Pozzuoli in the unstable belt of Italy

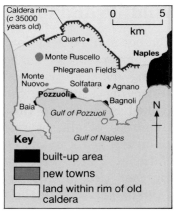

Figure B (*below*) A disaster history of Pozzuoli

Date	Events
BC	
4500	Major volcanic eruption. Caused devastation for 50 square kilometres round about Pozzuoli
AD	
79	Eruption of nearby Mount Vesuvius, burying Roman towns of Pompeii and Herculaneum in ash and mud
	Roman town of Pozzuoli begins to sink
1198	Eruption of nearby Mount Solfatara, destroying medieval town of Pozzuoli
1530	Ground level begins to rise again
1538	Major eruption a mile from Pozzuoli, producing a 120 metre-high volcano in two days
1970	Ground level under Pozzuoli begins to rise again
1982	Authorities begin to evacuate parts of Pozzuoli

Figure C Newspaper report on Pozzuoli

Families flee from the 'gates of hell'

For over a year now, Pozzuoli has been rising by an average of about three millimetres a day. It is now three feet higher than it was in 1982 and still rising.

Buildings have begun to sway and crack. Well over half the population of 70 000 has abandoned the town, 20 000 of them for a temporary 'tent city' on its outskirts. Even from there they can hear clearly the ominous roars and bangs indicating intense volcanic activity. Scientists are not ruling out the possibility that Pozzuoli is about to become a new volcano, but cannot predict exactly what will happen when.

Pozzuoli is in the middle of a huge, highly-active zone. Seen from the air, it is set in a lunar landscape of volcanic craters, most of them only apparently inactive. The Greeks and Romans called the area 'the flaming fields', because of its boiling springs and sulphur jets. They considered it the gateway to hell.

The upward movement of the earth – thought to be caused by the pressure of a swelling mass of molten rock about two or three miles below the surface – has left Pozzuoli's shallow harbour unnavigable for large ships, so the port is now practically deserted. The Italian Civil Protection Authority claims that 'everything is under control', though this is of little comfort to the inhabitants of Pozzuoli, who see their houses gradually collapsing under a daily barrage of earthquakes.

Thirty-five thousand years ago the top of a volcano was blown off in an eruption. The crater of the volcano became a *caldera*, or basin, measuring several kilometres across. The village of Pozzuoli lies within the rim of this caldera, a few kilometres along the coast from Naples in Italy (Figure A).

Since the caldera was formed there have been many other eruptions in the area, as Figure B shows. In 1983 engineers began to notice a considerably greater degree of seismic activity, leading to an earthquake which registered 4 on the Richter scale. Not surprisingly people have become very worried about the possibility of a further volcanic eruption (see Figure C). There may be as little as two hours warning.

Underneath Pozzuoli

The area inside the caldera rim is called the Phlegraean Fields. Geologists have noticed that many of the small cones and vents that have appeared inside this area in recent centuries lie close to Pozzuoli. This has made them think that the crust just beneath Pozzuoli may be the centre of the volcanic activity. They think that 2-3 km below the surface, bodies of magma are continually shifting in position. It is this instability which is causing the surface to heave upwards. The scientists are especially worried about what might happen if magma near the surface struck a water-bearing rock. If this happened the conversion of water into steam would produce a devastating explosion.

The effects of an eruption offshore could be even worse. Tsunamis or giant tidal waves would be generated instantly, causing massive destruction as they crashed onshore.

What is being done?

Despite the likelihood of a disaster the Italian government says it doesn't have enough money to spend on trying to predict future tremors. Since the damage to the town is now so bad, engineers have given up making repairs to buildings and now only record damage as it occurs. Over a third of the population has been evacuated. There are now over 30 000 refugees from the town living in campsites or lodgings, or with relatives in the nearby area. The town centre is deserted, all the shops closed down years ago. A new town for 20 000 people is being built at Monte Ruscello, 6 km from Pozzuoli and outside the worst danger zone.

People seem more concerned about the inconvenience than about the danger. They often make trips back to their old, deserted homes to pick up a few more belongings. Some people still live in the town. Others grumble about the poor compensation the state has agreed to pay them for losing their homes. The owners of holiday homes and hotels complain about how much tourist trade they have been losing.

Southern Italy – an unstable belt

Figure A shows why Pozzuoli is so vulnerable to a volcanic eruption. The whole of this part of Italy lies on a plate margin which separates the Eurasian and African plates. Along this boundary there has been a long history of disasters from earthquakes and volcanic activity. Look back to previous units to find out why plate margins produce these conditions.

Figure D A crack in the paving stones of a street in Pozzuoli

QUESTIONS

1 Where is Pozzuoli? Write a sentence giving its location as carefully as you can.

2 Use the extract and, the table and Figure D:
   a) Why did the Romans call this area 'the flaming fields'?
   b) Give *four* reasons why people think a major volcanic eruption may occur at Pozzuoli.
   c) Explain why:
      i)   The ruins of ancient Pozzuoli sank beneath the sea;
      ii) The harbour of Pozzuoli is now unusable.
   d) 'Everything is under control'. Do you agree? Give reasons for your answer.

Answer *either* question 3 *or* question 4.

3 Read the four courses of action below. Which do you think the civil authorities should follow? Give reasons for your choice.
   a) Immediate mass evacuation and resettlement.
   b) Make all buildings earthquake-proof.
   c) Try to predict a disaster more precisely, and then evacuate.
   d) Do nothing until a disaster occurs.

or

4 a) You are a refugee from Pozzuoli living in the new settlement at Monte Ruscello. Write a letter to the Italian government complaining about how it has been handling the problem, and stating your fears for the future.
   b) Swap letters with your neighbour. Now change roles. You are a representative of the Italian government. You and your neighbour should read each other's letter. Write a reply to your neighbour's letter explaining the Italian government's policy.

Unit 2 ASSESSMENT

What you know

Study Figure A, which shows zones in which earthquakes and active volcanoes occur.

1 Use an atlas to find out which of the following countries are in the zones shown on the map:
Brazil   Nigeria   Cyprus   Philippines (2 marks)

2 Which of **1**, **2**, **3**, and **4** on Figure A represent the following?

the Nazca plate   Mount St Helens
Pozzuoli   the San Andreas fault   (2 marks)

3 **a)** Draw a diagram to illustrate an anticline.
b) Explain how an anticline forms.
c) Name a location in Britain where the rocks are heavily folded.
d) Explain how folding in rocks can make mining difficult.   (12 marks)

4 **a)** Name a location in North America where a major Volcanic eruption took place in 1983.
b) Describe its effects on the area's wildlife.   (6 marks)

5 Explain how plate movement produces earthquakes.
(4 marks)

6 Mount St Helens and Pozzuoli are examples of volcanic activity which have affected people's lives.
a) Why are more people affected by Pozzuoli than by Mount St Helens?
b) Give an example of a local person's reaction to the Pozzuoli volcanic problem.
c) Find a reaction to the Mount St Helens eruption from a local person which shows a different point of view from b.   (9 marks)

7 Give some reasons why so many people live in unstable areas despite the hazards involved.   (5 marks)

Figure B Report in the *Guardian*, July 1985

Britain shocked by earthquake

Large areas of Britain and the east coast of the Irish Republic were struck yesterday by the most severe earthquake in the area for at least 50 years.

The shocks, which were registered as far away as Norway and France, measured 5.5 on the Richter scale. The epicentre of the quake was probably around the North Wales fishing village of Porthmadog.

Hundreds of incidents were reported to the emergency services.

Power failed at Pwllheli, high rise buildings at Swansea were evacuated, and thousands of homes were rocked in Liverpool. The effects were felt as far south as Somerset and the top floors of a tower block in Bristol were evacuated when the building began to rock.

The tremor in Blaenau Ffestinog lasted about 45 seconds, during which many people, some still in their nightclothes, left shaking houses to gather in the streets. Observers said that the quake, shortly before 8 a.m., rattled around the mountains and swept through the quarrying town with what seemed supernatural force.

Several buildings swayed in the shock but property casualties were limited mainly to chimney pots which toppled to the ground.

Gas boards, throughout the affected areas asked consumers to be particularly vigilant in reporting any escapes.

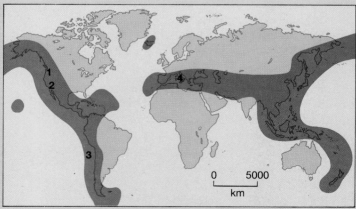

Figure A Zones of earthquake and volcanic activity

Key
Zones in which many earthquakes and active volcanoes occur

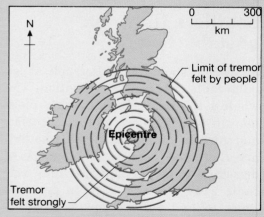

Figure C The area affected by the 1985 earthquake

What you understand

Look back at page 16 and reread the extract about the San Francisco earthquake in California. Compare it with Figures B and C on this page which refer to an earthquake in Wales.

1 Compare the two earthquakes in respect of:
   a) their strengths
   b) their effects on people   (6 marks)

2 Explain why you might expect an earthquake to occur in California but you might not expect an earthquake in Wales.   (4 marks)

3 What does the information on the Welsh earthquake tell you about:
   a) how an earthquake shock spreads?
   b) how the place of origin of an earthquake can be identified?   (6 marks)

4 What suggests to you that people do not always respond to natural hazards in the same way?   (4 marks)

5 'People in north Wales have to live with the risk of earthquakes.' Do you agree with this? Give reasons for your answer.   (5 marks)
                                        Total: 25 marks

What you can do

1 Choose an area of the world which experiences regular earthquake and volcanic activity. Ask your teacher where you can find information about volcanoes and earthquakes which have occurred in this region.
                                          (5 marks)

2 Draw a map for this region showing plate boundaries. Use an atlas to plot the location of the volcanoes and earthquakes.   (5 marks)

3 Measure the distance between each volcano or earthquake location and the plate boundary.   (5 marks)

4 Draw up a table to show the number of volcano or earthquake locations which are:
   a) on plate boundaries,
   b) close to plate boundaries
   c) distant from plate boundaries   (5 marks)

5 Write a short essay describing and explaining your findings.   (5 marks)
                                        Total: 25 marks

Details for pupil profile sheets Unit 2

Knowledge and understanding

1 Plate tectonics
2 Continental drift
3 Processes of rock formation
4 Processes of faulting, folding
5 Processes of earthquake causation
6 Earthquake measurement
7 Effects of earthquakes on people
8 Volcanic processes
9 Effects of volcanic activity on the landscape
10 Effects of volcanic activity on people

Skills

1 Determining the character of plate margins from map evidence
2 Drawing maps to show relationships between different types of data
3 Making decisions on mine location from data provided
4 Reading information from a map
5 Plotting earthquake location from data provided
6 Accurate copying of selected features from a map
7 Writing letter clearly expressing views on an issue
8 Summarising data from text and diagrams in the form of a table
9 Producing written summary of results of tasks carried out

Values

1 Awareness of benefits and problems of unstable environments to man
2 Awareness of how natural hazards are viewed by people who live close to them

Unit 3: Sculpturing the landscape

The stone building in Figure A has been partly cleaned. Over the years, soot and dirt from the atmosphere had gradually blackened the surface. Careful cleaning restores the original colour.

Besides discolouring it, the atmosphere also attacks stone. Acids in rainwater decompose minerals present in the stone. The surface is gradually worn away. Finely carved details may become unrecognisable. Restoration is very costly.

Weathering of rocks

Natural rock surfaces are weathered in the same way. Freshly cut stone from a quarry is always a lighter, cleaner colour than the stone which has been exposed to the atmosphere for a long time. This is because the exposed limestone is constantly attacked by carbonic acid. This acid is always present in rainwater and cloud droplets, and comes from the carbon dioxide in the atmosphere. When it attacks limestone it washes calcium minerals away in solution and leaves the surface darker.

Sulphuric acid is also found in the atmosphere. This comes from the sulphur dioxide given out by car exhausts, coal fires, and power station emissions.

Figure A The contrast between cleaned and uncleaned stone

Figure B Types of chemical weathering

Figure C A limestone pavement in Yorkshire with lichens and plants growing on it

Figure D How chemical, biological and mechanical weathering act together

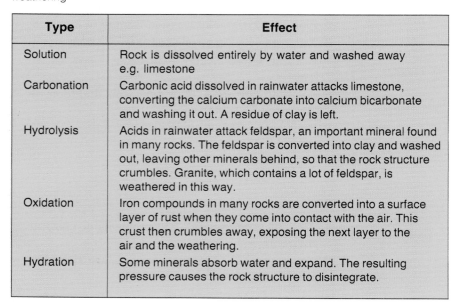

Type	Effect
Solution	Rock is dissolved entirely by water and washed away e.g. limestone
Carbonation	Carbonic acid dissolved in rainwater attacks limestone, converting the calcium carbonate into calcium bicarbonate and washing it out. A residue of clay is left.
Hydrolysis	Acids in rainwater attack feldspar, an important mineral found in many rocks. The feldspar is converted into clay and washed out, leaving other minerals behind, so that the rock structure crumbles. Granite, which contains a lot of feldspar, is weathered in this way.
Oxidation	Iron compounds in many rocks are converted into a surface layer of rust when they come into contact with the air. This crust then crumbles away, exposing the next layer to the air and the weathering.
Hydration	Some minerals absorb water and expand. The resulting pressure causes the rock structure to disintegrate.

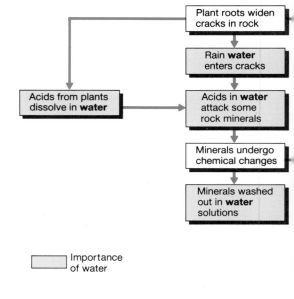

Plant roots widen cracks in rock

Rain **water** enters cracks

Acids from plants dissolve in **water**

Acids in **water** attack some rock minerals

Minerals undergo chemical changes

Minerals washed out in **water** solutions

Importance of water

It attacks a range of minerals in rocks, converting them into other minerals which are washed away by rainwater. Figure B lists some of the chemical processes that take place when rocks are weathered.

When you look more closely at rock surfaces, you often find them covered with a thin layer of mosses, algae or lichens. These grow well in cracks and crevices. The plants contain water, and when they die the water becomes slightly acidic and begins to attack the rock minerals. The roots of plants growing in cracks and joints in the rock (Figure C) also exert pressure on the sides of the cracks, widening them. This allows more water to enter the cracks to attack them chemically.

Weathering and temperature

In mountain areas the temperature falls by 1° C for every 100 metre increase in height. On higher slopes the temperature often falls below freezing at night. Water in cracks expands as it freezes, exerting great pressure on the rock, which shatters into angular pieces. These fragments collect around the base of the slope in heaps of angular boulders called *scree* or *talus*. In moun-tain areas this *frost shattering* is likely to be going on for much of the year.

Types of weathering

Weathering may be *chemical, biological,* or *mechanical.* It is important to remember that the different types act together rather than separately. Figure D shows how one type of weathering makes it easy for another to get started. Notice also how important water is to weathering. Without some water present very little weathering can take place at all.

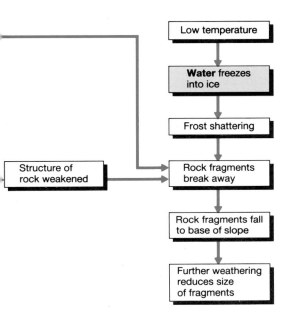

QUESTIONS

1 From the text and figures, find:
   a) *two* ways the effects of weathering might be seen in a town
   b) *two* ways plants and vegetation cause weathering of rocks
   c) *three* ways in which water contributes to weathering.
   d) *three* processes which produce rock fragments.
   e) *two* consequences of chemical changes to minerals.

2 Study the Figure C:
   a) Describe and explain the weathering processes which are now taking place on this surface.
   b) What would be the effects on weathering if the climate became
   i drier?   ii colder?

3 **Fieldwork**
   Look at a number of gravestones in a cemetery or churchyard. Note the dates on the gravestones and try to assess the amount of weathering that has taken place on each gravestone. Use the table below as a guide:

Weathering category	Degree of weathering	Evidence on gravestone
1	Unweathered	Surface clean, letters sharp
2	Slight weathering	Faint rounding of corners of letters
3	Moderate weathering	Rough surface but letters readable
4	Very bad weathering	Letters almost unreadable
5	Extreme weathering	No letters left, scaling

   a) Are the older gravestones more weathered than the newer ones? How much weathering has taken place on stones which are:
   i) 50 years old?   ii) a hundred years old?
   b) Try to find out what the stones are made of. Do some types of stone weather more easily than others?

The shape of the land

In hot deserts, temperatures may reach over 40° C by day but can fall to below freezing at night. Minerals in rocks are constantly expanding and contracting at different rates. The result is that mineral crystals and grains begin to fall out of the rocks, so that the structure of the rock is weakened. This is called *granular disintegration*.

Figure A shows part of the desert of the south-west United States. Notice the long straight slopes, with sharp breaks between them. The landscape is very angular in appearance. Here there is little water, and so chemical weathering is unimportant (see Figure D). The rocks are shaped mainly by the mechanical disintegration brought about by the intense heat of the day and cold at night. Compare the desert landscape in Figure A with Figure B, which shows a downland area of England. The gentle curves of the downs are mostly a result of chemical weathering.

Slopes and contours

The sketches in Figure C show some slopes and landforms of different shapes and how they look as contour maps. Each contour pattern is a sort of fingerprint of the slopes or landform. With practice we can look at the contour patterns and describe the slope or the landform. We may also be able to say something about the sorts of weathering processes that are at work on it.

Figure A The desert landscape of Monument Valley, Arizona, USA

Figure B The South Downs near Lewes, Sussex

Types of desert

Erg	Saharan name for large areas of sand. Only about 25 per cent of the desert surface is erg.
Serir	Gravel, stones and rock boulders
Hamada	Bare mountains and craggy rock surfaces. Most of the Sahara is hamada

Weathering in deserts
Mainly mechanical by water and wind, producing angular landscapes

Water erosion
Although deserts are very dry, some rain does fall and water erosion is responsible for the main features of desert landscapes such as:

* **wadis** – deep gorges which become temporary rivers during storms

* **buttes** – stumps of mountains and rock masses which have been mostly worn away

* **pediments** – smooth, bare, gently sloping rock surfaces planed off by water

* **fans** – built up alluvium washed out of wadis

Wind erosion
Weathered rock material in the form of dust and sand is transported by the wind

* rocks are sandblasted into peculiar shapes such as **pedestal rocks**

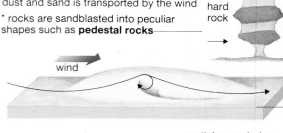

hard rock

wind

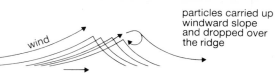

wind

particles carried up windward slope and dropped over the ridge

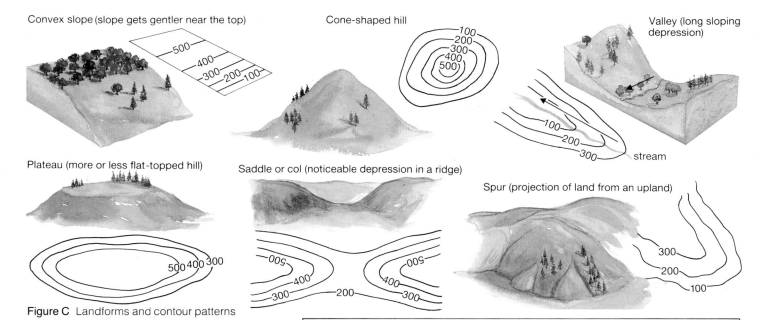

Convex slope (slope gets gentler near the top)

Cone-shaped hill

Valley (long sloping depression)

stream

Plateau (more or less flat-topped hill)

Saddle or col (noticeable depression in a ridge)

Spur (projection of land from an upland)

Figure C Landforms and contour patterns

Figure D Desert landforms

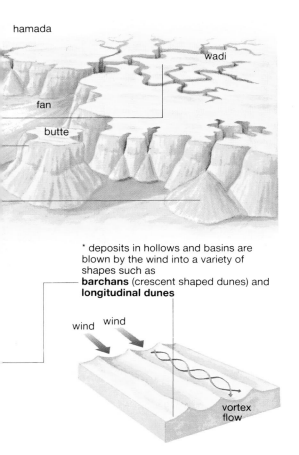

hamada

wadi

fan

butte

* deposits in hollows and basins are blown by the wind into a variety of shapes such as
barchans (crescent shaped dunes) and
longitudinal dunes

wind   wind

vortex flow

QUESTIONS

Questions 1 and 2 refer to the OS map extract on page 126.

1 A party of students walked along the section of footpath between Grid References 437474 and 400460. One student recorded the following account in a field-work note-book. Copy the extract and use the map to help you fill in the blanks.

'The path climbed steeply from the minor road at 437474. After about a kilometre we crossed the .... of Bwlch Mawr. The path here is at .... metres high. On our right the slopes were covered in boulders called .... These boulders were formed by the type of weathering called .... About 1.5 km further on, the path descended into a .... between two hills. When we reached 400460 we had walked .... km, or about .... miles.'

2 **a)** The figure below is a cross-section between two points on the map. Copy and complete it.
b) Now insert the correct letter into the boxes from the key below.
A View of a cone-shaped hill with scree on the steep upper slopes.
B A uniform but steep slope where soil creep is likely to happen.
C A saddle or col between several hills.
D The spur of a hill with cliff faces exposed to frost shattering.

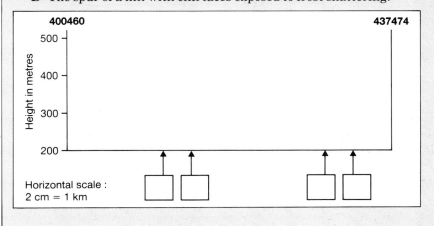

400460   437474

Height in metres

500

400

300

200

Horizontal scale :
2 cm = 1 km

Figure A Climbing on screes can be dangerous. These walkers are in a fan formation to lessen the risks

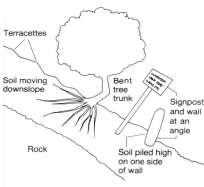

Figure B Signs of soil creep on a hillslope

The walkers shown in Figure A are on a scree. This is a pile of boulders formed from the *frost* shattering of the mountain slopes higher up. Because the scree is made of loose boulders it is very unstable. The steep angle of the scree also makes it dangerous to walk on.

Steep, loose slopes like screes are not the only ones that are unstable. Gentle slopes covered with soil and vegetation may also move, even if only very slowly. Figure B shows some of the signs of *soil creep*. Look out for them the next time you walk in the countryside. On particularly steep slopes the soil might form regular ridges called *terracettes* across the angle of slope. People sometimes call these 'sheep walks' but they are formed by soil creep, not by sheep.

Slope failure

Unstable slopes may also suffer *slope failure*. The surface soil and rocks break away from the main mass and slip or slide to the bottom of the slope. This happens because the slope is subjected to stress. There is always some stress on a slope caused by the force of gravity. Stress may be increased by the slope becoming saturated with rainwater, or by tremors caused by earthquakes or quarrying. If this happens the stress exceeds the natural 'strength' of the slope, and failure occurs. In January 1989 a number of villages in Tadzhikistan in the USSR were engulfed by landslides after an earthquake.

CASE STUDY 1: Yungay, Peru, 1970

An earthquake shock triggered off the collapse of an ice-cap on the peak of Mount Huascaran. This produced a debris flow of snow, rock, mud and ice which surged down the valley at 320 km per hour. It took four minutes to reach the town of Yungay, which it completely destroyed. Only 92 people survived out of a population of 25 000. An eye-witness said:

'The crest of the wave had a curl, like a huge breaker coming in from the ocean. I

CASE STUDY 2: Aberfan, Wales, 1966

Aberfan is a mining village. During many years of coal mining, huge heaps of mining waste had become piled up high on to the valley sides overlooking the village. Heavy rain caused the upper part of the tip to become saturated and to break away from the main mass. A tongue of black mud flowed down on to the village 250 metres below, covering the school and killing most of the village's children.

An investigation afterwards showed that for thirty years mining waste had been tipped on the hillside across a line of springs. The tip had been saturated with water for a long time, and it only needed a storm to trigger off the slip. The stress turned the waste into a liquid mass.

A view of Aberfan at the time of the disaster in October 1966

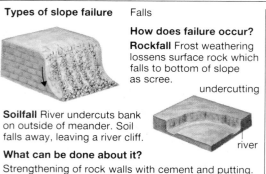

Types of slope failure Falls

How does failure occur?
Rockfall Frost weathering lossens surface rock which falls to bottom of slope as scree.

Soilfall River undercuts bank on outside of meander. Soil falls away, leaving a river cliff.

What can be done about it?
Strengthening of rock walls with cement and putting. anchor bolts in place.
Covering rock with steel mesh.
Creating benches or terraces in rock wall.
Diverting river channels to prevent soilfall.

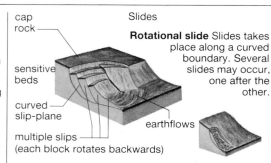

Slides

Rotational slide Slides takes place along a curved boundary. Several slides may occur, one after the other.

What can be done about it?
Making terraces or benches to flatten the slope.
Draining off surface water via ditches or pipes under the surface.

estimated the wave to be at least 80 metres high. I saw hundreds of people running in all directions. All the while, there was a continuous roar and rumble. I was only 10 seconds ahead of it. It was the most horrible thing I have ever experienced, and I will never forget it.'

Crosses mark the graves of some of the victims of the Yungay disaster

CASE STUDY 3: Dowlands, Axmouth, Devon, 1839

Along this stretch of coast the cliffs are made of chalk and sandstone on a clay base. Here after a period of heavy rain, a part of the cliff broke away and slid seawards. The slippage had been caused by the clay becoming saturated and unable to support the cliff. It produced a chasm 400 metres wide. Several houses were carried along with the slippage.

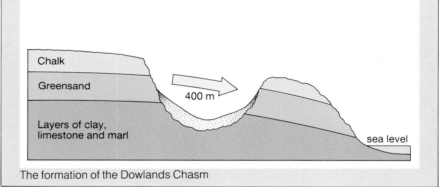

The formation of the Dowlands Chasm

Flows

Earthflow or mudflow
Loose material becomes saturated with water and begins to flow downslope.

Sand run Flow or dry sand from a sandy cliff

What can be done about it?
Sealing the surface to prevent water seeping in.
Placing supports of rock at foot of slope.
Drilling pilings through soil into sold rock beneath.

QUESTIONS

1 Give two characteristics of a scree.

2 Explain why slopes may fail.

3 Study the three case studies on Yungay, Aberfan and Dowlands:
  a) Answer the following:
   i) Which event was the most disastrous for people?
   ii) Which could have been most easily prevented?
  b) 'Water plays a major part in slope failure'. What evidence can you find to support this view?
  c) Put yourself in the position of someone attending an enquiry into the Aberfan disaster. You now have to write a report for the public summarising the enquiry's findings. Write a summary of the main points you will include under the headings of:
   i) Why the disaster occurred
   ii) What should be done to prevent similar disasters.

Unit 3 ASSESSMENT

Make yourself a slope surveying instrument or 'pantometer'. This is made of two uprights loosely bolted together with cross-pieces. A protractor and spirit level are fitted to one end, as shown in Figure A. Use the pantometer for the following fieldwork.

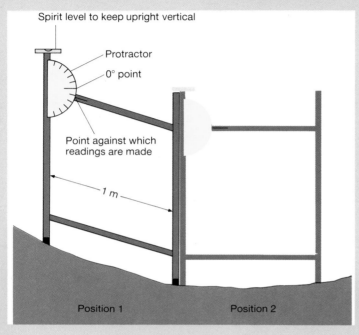

Spirit level to keep upright vertical

Protractor

0° point

Point against which readings are made

1 m

Position 1   Position 2

Figure A How a pantometer is made

Fieldwork

1 Find a long hillslope with marked 'breaks' of slope. Note: make sure your teacher knows where you are working. Never work on a scree or a cliff.
   a) Start at the top of the slope. Place the pantometer on the slope so that the spirit level keeps the uprights vertical. Measure the angle of slope from the horizontal using the protractor. Record this in your notebook.
   b) Move down the slope five paces and repeat the exercise. Record the slope angle every five paces down the slope.
   c) As you work, look for signs of slope instability or failure, and record them.
   d) Produce a slope profile from your data, similar to Figure B. Label the profile with the signs of instability you observed.

2 Use your results to test and discuss the following ideas:
   a) Many hillslopes are made up of several elements or surfaces at different angles.
   b) Curving slopes are more common than straight, angular slopes.
   c) Exposed rock surfaces often cause steep, straight slopes.

6°   11 m

12 m

Working downslope

29°

2°   15 m

10 m

13°

0   5
m

Slope angle from protractor reading

Figure B A student's slope profile drawn from pantometer measurements

3 Write up the results of this work as a *fieldwork report* under these headings.

Aims: what the tasks aimed to do.   (10 marks)
Methods: the way the tasks were carried out   (15 marks)
Findings: studying the data collected   (20 marks)
Conclusions: related to the original aims   (5 marks)

                                        Total: 40 marks

How to write a good report

All the effort and planning that goes into fieldwork may be wasted if you don't present your findings properly. These are a number of things to remember:

1 Your final report must be well planned and laid out

2 Organise your report under the following headings:
   a) **Aims** – set out what you are going to try to do
   b) **Methods** – describe how you carried out the task you set yourself
   c) **Findings** – present clearly the data you have collected using diagrams, maps, tables, photographs, etc.
   d) **Conclusions** – summarize what you have found out. Point out any problems , the reasons for them and suggest solutions to the problems

3 Make sure all your diagrams, maps, tables, etc are meaningful and not just for decoration

4 Make your report as attractive and tidy as possible.

Details for pupil profile sheets Unit 3

Knowledge and understanding

1 Processes causing weathering – mechanical, chemical, biological.
2 Types of chemical weathering
3 Importance of water and climate in weathering.
4 Role of weathering in slope development.
5 Causes of slope instability and failure.

Skills

1 Assessing weathering from gravestones.
2 Drawing of cross-section from an Ordnance Survey map.
3 Recognising relief features on Ordnance Survey maps.
4 Construction of pantometer.
5 Using pantometer to construct a slope profile.
6 Writing a fieldwork report.

Values

1 Awareness of importance of weathering for the 'built environment'.
2 Awareness of how slope failure can be a hazard for people

Unit 4: Water over all

Your household water amenities operate as a *system* (Figure A). A feature of a system is that materials and energy are constantly circulating through it. At home water moves through a network of pipes. There is an *input* into the system (hot and cold water) and an *output* from it (waste water). Within the system, water is held in various *stores* (tanks and boilers). The system is self-contained, so that if the Water Board cut off your supply, the water supply of other houses is not affected.

Your domestic water system is only a tiny part of a much bigger system which distributes water from reservoirs to homes and other buildings, and then takes the waste water away to the sewage works for purification. This system in turn fits into a bigger one. This is called the *hydrological system* or *hydrological cycle* (see Figure B). Answer question 1 before you carry on with this unit.

The amount of water within the earth's hydrological cycle remains constant at about 1384 million cubic kilometres. It circulates all the time on or close to the earth's surface in the form of streams, rivers, water vapour, and rainfall (or snow). Movements of water within the hydrological cycle derive

Figure A A household water system

Figure B The hydrological cycle, (*inset*) flow diagram of the hydrological cycle

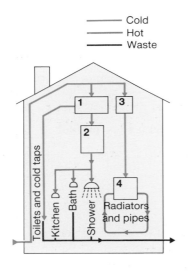

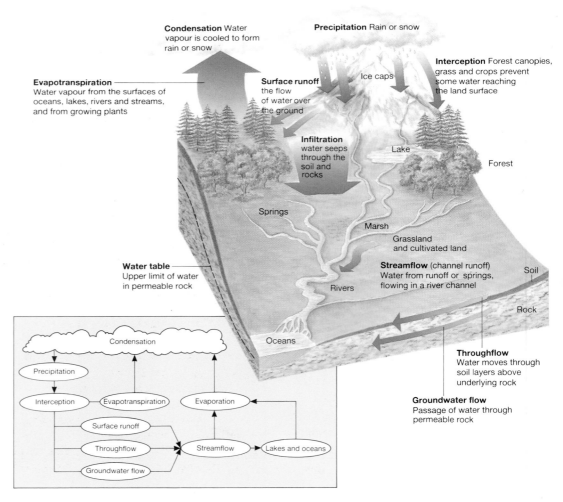

some energy from the sun (evaporation) or from gravity (stream movements). The hydrological cycle contains various stores – clouds, ponds, lakes, and especially the oceans.

Figure C shows that the seas are by far the biggest store, containing over 97 per cent of the earth's moisture. Most of the remaining water is held frozen in the ice caps of Greenland and Antarctica and is effectively 'out of circulation' in the hydrological cycle. The greater part of what is left is in permeable rocks underground and may never come to the surface. Only a very small part of the earth's moisture is available to flow through the different stores of the hydrological cycle.

Water and people

Water is mankind's most important resource. As users of water, people step into the hydrological cycle and become part of it. Look at the hydrological cycle (Figure B) again and try to think of points on the diagram where you could insert different types of human use. Which parts of the cycle do you think we are most likely to be able to control?

Overall there is enough fresh water circulating through the hydrological cycle to meet the demands of about twice the existing world population. Its rate of use however varies enormously around the world (see Figure D) and it is not always found where people need it. To maintain a reasonable quality of life we need about 80 litres of water each every day.

There are some parts of the hyrological cycle which it is unlikely that people will ever be able to control. Despite some successful scientific experiments we will probably never be able to create rain artificially on a large scale. Although people can control some parts of the hydrological cycle in certain places, it is solar energy which controls the cycle as a whole.

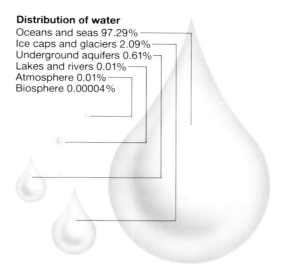

Distribution of water
Oceans and seas 97.29%
Ice caps and glaciers 2.09%
Underground aquifers 0.61%
Lakes and rivers 0.01%
Atmosphere 0.01%
Biosphere 0.00004%

Figure C The distribution of the earth's water

Figure D Domestic use of water around the world

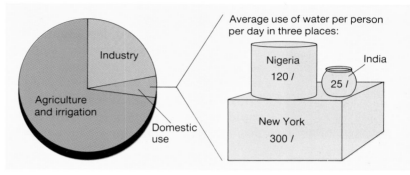

Average use of water per person per day in three places:
Industry
Agriculture and irrigation
Domestic use
Nigeria 120 /
India 25 /
New York 300 /

QUESTIONS

1 Make a simple copy of the domestic water system picture. On your copy label the *input* and *output*. Identify and label the four *stores* from the list below:
   central heating boiler   central heating header tank
   hot water tank   cold water tank

2 Study Figure B.
   a) Find a word which describes:
      i) how the atmosphere gains water from plants
      ii) how water percolates through the soil
      iii) the upper limit reached by water stored in rocks
   b) Describe *two* ways by which sub-surface water can find its way into streams, lakes or oceans.
   c) Give a reason why *surface runoff* is always likely to be less than *precipitation*.
   d) Complete these 'equations':
   i) Streamflow = ... + ... + infiltration
   ii) Surface runoff = precipitation − (............ + ...)

3 **a)** Draw a flow diagram in which: the *input* is precipitation and the *output* is discharge from a sewage works into a river.
   b) Complete the diagram to show what happens to the water in your 'system' between the input and the output. Include the following in your diagram:
      household use   a reservoir
      irrigation from a well   hydroelectricity generation

A natural umbrella

Sometimes you can avoid the worst of a shower of rain by sheltering under a tree. This is because some of the precipitation has been *intercepted* by the branches and leaves of the tree. Eventually the intercepted moisture will be returned to the atmosphere by *evaporation*. All plants intercept precipitation to some extent, even low growing forms like grasses or herbs. In a dense forest (Figure A) where the crowns of the trees form a continuous canopy, it may be many minutes after the start of a shower before any rain reaches the ground at all.

On a hot summer's day plants in a greenhouse will need very frequent watering. Without regular watering they will begin to wilt very quickly indeed. The need for water is caused by the rapid rate of *transpiration*. This is the loss of moisture to the air by evaporation from the surface tissues of the plant. Plants need to transpire so that they can draw up moisture from the soil through their roots. The soil moisture contains vital plant nutrients. In desert conditions many plants have adapted to retain water. Leaves have waxy surfaces, or are thorn-like (Figure B).

Water on the ground

Study Figure C. Notice the variations between slope gradient and the sort of ground cover. Try to imagine what happens when rain from a heavy shower falls on each type of surface.

Soil moisture

Infiltrating moisture is absorbed by the soil until the soil becomes saturated. Further moisture will then pass down

Figure A (*top*) Dense vegetation in a tropical rain forest in Costa Rica

Figure B (*above*) Scrub and cacti in the Arizona desert, USA

Figure C What happens to precipitation on different land surfaces

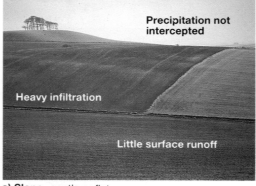

a) **Slope** gentle or flat
Land cover bare soil, no crops
Permeability high

b) **Slope** gentle or flat
Land cover woodland or crops
Permeability high

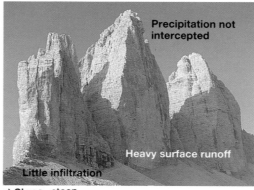

c) **Slope** steep
Land cover bare rock, little soil
Permeability very low

d) **Slope** gentle or flat
Land cover buildings, roads, driveways, car parks, gardens and parkland
Permeability mostly low

through the soil to the bedrock beneath. In areas of regular rainfall moisture is continually *percolating* downwards.

In the summer of 1976 Britain had one of its worst droughts for decades. There was so little precipitation and infiltration that the soil began to dry out. In many areas, crops wilted because there was not enough moisture in the soil to replace the water by transpiration. Public water supplies became a national problem because reservoir levels fell so low. When the dry spell ended it took several weeks before normal soil moisture levels returned. It took even longer for reservoirs to refill.

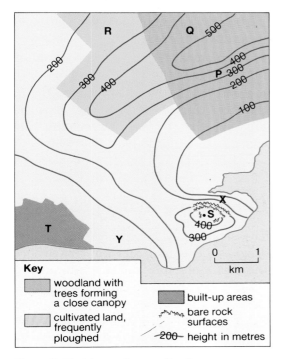

Figure D Sketch map for question 3

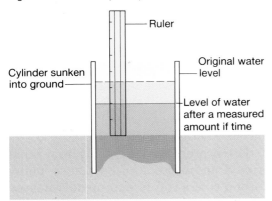

Figure E How to measure infiltration

QUESTIONS

1 Find a term that describes:
   a) loss of moisture by plants to the air
   b) leaves and branches of plants retaining rainwater
   c) water draining down a slope

2 Explain how each of the following may affect the normal pattern of water movements:
   a) a large car park
   b) a long period of drought
   c) felling an area of woodland

3 Study Figure D:
   a) Copy these statements choosing the correct answers:
      i) Interception at **Q** is likely to be very heavy/significant/unimportant
      ii) Infiltration at **P** is likely to be very heavy/significant/unimportant
      iii) Surface runoff at **R** is likely to be very heavy/significant/unimportant
   b) Name a location on the map where:
      i) Runoff is more important than interception
      ii) Human activity is causing heavy runoff
      iii) Human activity is assisting infiltration
      Give reasons for your answers.
   c) For location **S** produce a sketch diagram to show the relationship between interception, infiltration, and runoff.
   d) Locations **X** and **Y** are being considered as alternative sites for a holiday village. Write a report comparing the drainage characteristics of each site.

   Fieldwork

4 *A project to show transpiration*
   Cover a leafy branch with a large polythene bag. Tie it at the base to make it watertight. Leave it for a day. Tip the water from the bag into a measuring cylinder. Read off the amount of water collected.
   Repeat the experiment on other days, with different weather. Does the amount of transpiration vary with temperature or sunshine?

5 b) *A project to show infiltration*
   Obtain a cylinder about 30 cm long. A piece of plastic drainpipe will do. Knock the cylinder about 10 cm into the ground. Pour a measured quantity of water into the cylinder until it is nearly full. Immediately note the height of water in the cylinder with a ruler (Figure E).
   Record the drop in water level, at first every minute, then at longer intervals over an hour or so. Plot your results on a graph of time/infiltration rate (mm per hour).
   Repeat the experiment at different sites. Discuss how your variations in infiltration rates might be caused by:
      i) soil wetness
      ii) soil compactness

Figure A shows the *drainage basin* or *catchment* of a river. Some rain which falls within the basin may be intercepted and returned to the atmosphere by evaporation, or it may be absorbed by the soil and transpired by growing plants into the air.

The remaining moisture will eventually reach the river system by various routes:

- runoff directly into the river's tributary streams
- infiltration through the soil, with seepage out to the surface lower down the slope
- percolation through permeable rocks as ground water, coming to the surface elsewhere as springs.

Figure A The drainage basin of a river with hydrographs showing runoff at three places

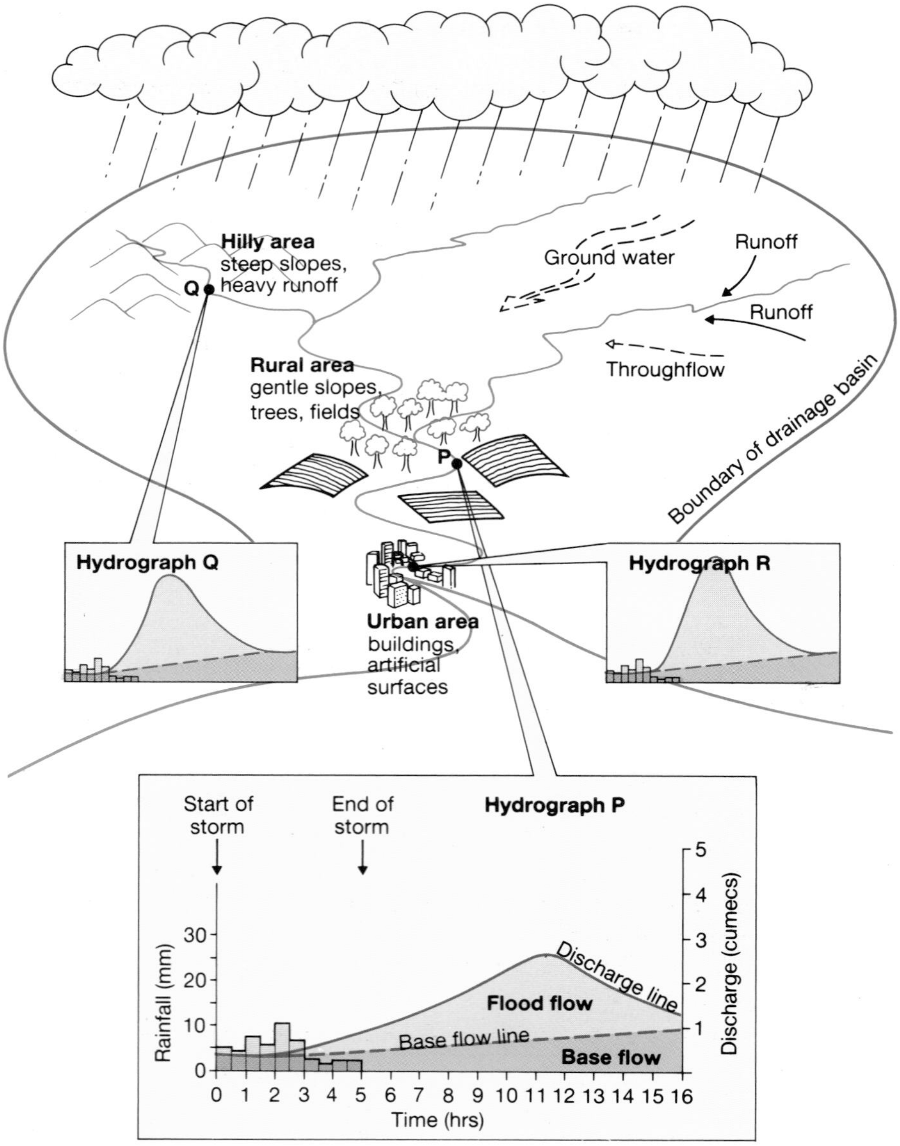

A hydrograph

The graph for location P on Figure A is called a *hydrograph*. It shows how rainfall influences river flow within a drainage basin. On the hydrograph the bars show the amount of rainfall recorded at hourly periods.

The red line shows how the *discharge* or volume of water in the river changed during and after the storm. The discharge was measured in units called *cumecs* at the points shown on the river in the diagram. All the rainwater which infiltrated into the basin above point P eventually passed through it as *streamflow* or *channel runoff*.

The hydrograph distinguishes between two different types of discharge:

- *base flow* is the water there would be in the river without the storm
- *flood flow* is the amount of water in the river caused by the storm. It is the area on the graph between the discharge line and the base-flow line.

Comparing hydrographs

The streamflow measurements for hydrograph P came from an area where there is more infiltration than surface runoff. The hydrograph shows a slow but steady rise in river discharge, with long lag time between peak rainfall and discharge. This is called a *steady response*.

For hydrograph Q, a tributary of the river was measured in a hilly area where there is little infiltration but a lot of runoff. Notice the difference this makes to the hydrograph. There is a much quicker rise in discharge. This is a *flash response* and leads to floods. Urban conditions also produce flash floods (hydrograph R and Figure B).

Other problems can result from rapid runoff in urban areas because many urban rivers run in man-made concrete channels. These are smooth and allow the water to flow very fast. As the water surges downstream it can undermine

Hydrograph Q

Hilly area
steep slopes,
Q heavy runoff

Ground water   Runoff

Rural area
gentle slopes,
trees, fields   Runoff

Throughflow

P

Boundary of drainage basin

Urban area
buildings,
artificial
surfaces

Hydrograph R

Hydrograph P

Start of storm   End of storm

Discharge line

Flood flow

Base flow line

Base flow

Rainfall (mm) / Discharge (cumecs)

Time (hrs)

Figure B Flash flooding in Belsize Park, London

Figure C Rainfall and flood data for 16–18 August 1977 in the Brent drainage basin

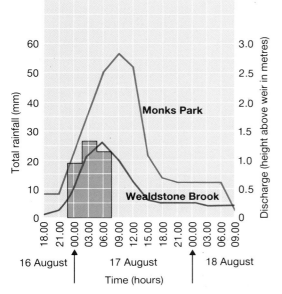

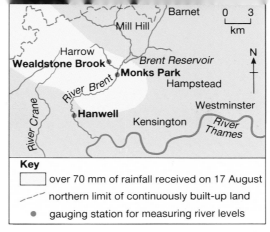

Figure D The Brent drainage basin

bridge supports, erode the banks faster, and spill over on to nearby farmland. Some town councils have developed flood prevention programmes (see below).

Some flood prevention measures

- widening and deepening artificial river channels to take more water
- increasing capacity of weirs
- using low-lying parks, golf courses, etc. as 'washlands'; in these areas nothing is done to stop flooding; this in turn helps to stop floods in the built-up areas
- building embankments around the washlands to stop floodwaters spilling out
- enlarging drains under roads

QUESTIONS

1 Study the hydrograph P in Figure A and then answer the following:
   a) i) For how many hours did rainfall increase after the start of the storm?
     ii) How long did the storm last?
     iii) How many hours did it take for discharge to reach a peak?

2 State *two* differences between a steady response and a flash response.
   a) How long did it take for the flood flow to subside (for the river to return to its normal level)?
   b) Answer questions **a)** and **b)** for hydrograph R.

3 The hydrograph in Figure C shows rainfall and flood data for the storms of 16–18 August 1977 in the Brent drainage basin in north-west London. The flood data was collected at Wealdstone Brook and Monks Park. Further data is provided below for Hanwell.

Flood data for Hanwell, 16–18 August 1977 (from *Settlement,* Huggett and Meyer)

Date	Time (hours)	Height above weir (in metres)	Date	Time (hours)	Height above weir (in metres)
16/8	1800	0.5	17/8	1500	3.0
	2100	0.5		1800	2.5
17/8	0000	0.7		2100	1.5
	0300	1.8	18/8	0000	1.0
	0600	2.3		0300	0.9
	0900	3.0		0600	0.8
	1200	3.3		0900	0.8

a) Make of copy of the hydrograph. On the graph plot the discharge data for Hanwell.
b) What is the time difference between highest rainfall and highest discharge at (i) Wealdstone Brook? (ii) Hanwell?
c) Why is this time difference greater further downstream?
d) What effect do you think the Brent reservoir will have had on discharge downstream?
e) Which places along the Brent were most at risk from floods? Justify your answer.

4 'Floods are often caused as much by people as they are by heavy rain.'

List all the evidence you can find to support this view.

The North Downs (see Figure A) are made of chalk, which is a *permeable* rock. Permeable rocks allow water to pass into them and through them. On the North Downs most precipitation quickly sinks into the chalk, and so there is very little surface runoff. Water held in permeable rocks is called *ground water*. When the water reaches the base of the chalk it encounters the impermeable rocks beneath the chalk, and so cannot sink further. In this way the chalk acts as a water-retentive rock or *aquifer*.

Springs

In southern England the outcrops of chalk form *escarpments* or ridges with one steep slope (scarp slope) and one gentle or back slope (dip slope). Try to imagine what happens when the model chalk outcrop (see Figure A) gradually fills with water. As the water level or *water table* rises, the water will eventually find an outlet along the boundaries with adjoining rocks. By doing this the water will reach the surface as *springs*.

Springs form the sources of many streams in downland country, and have also been important points for settlement. Along the feet of downland escarpments are lines of springs which have given rise to 'spring-line' villages.

Artesian basins

The map in Figure A shows how the chalk extends under the whole of south-eastern England to form a basin with its edges as the Chilterns and North Downs. Within this basin the chalk is covered by much younger rocks. The rain which falls on these areas soaks into the chalk and gradually percolates further down the basin. In this way the chalk underneath the London area acts as a huge reservoir or *artesian basin*. Where wells are sunk deep enough they will penetrate the water table and the water may reach the surface under its own pressure. Artesian water from the chalk is a major source of water supply for the urbanised south-east of England.

Figure A Chalk and limestone areas of the UK

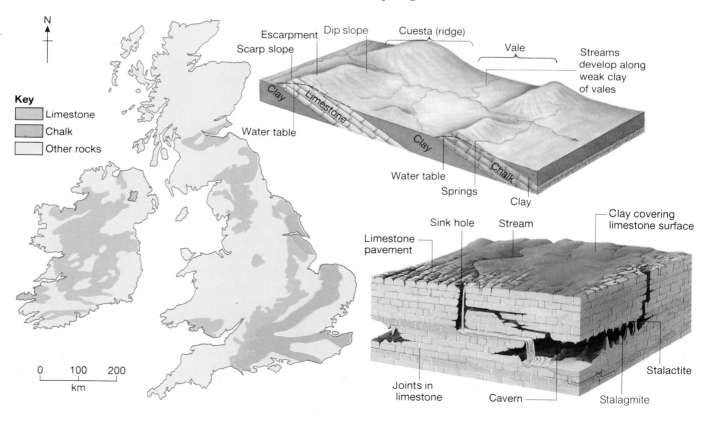

N

Key
- Limestone
- Chalk
- Other rocks

0   100   200
km

Escarpment
Scarp slope
Dip slope
Cuesta (ridge)
Vale
Streams develop along weak clay of vales
Clay
Limestone
Water table
Clay
Water table
Springs
Chalk
Clay

Sink hole
Stream
Clay covering limestone surface
Limestone pavement
Joints in limestone
Cavern
Stalagmite
Stalactite

Limestone pavements

Chalk is a soft, fine-grained form of limestone. Another type, Carboniferous or 'mountain' limestone, is harder. Mountain limestone forms large areas of upland, particularly in the Peak District and in the northern Pennines.

Like chalk, mountain limestone is permeable, and so its surface is usually dry. In some places it forms bare rock surfaces called pavements (see Figure C, page 26). The surface is carved up into deep fissures (*grykes*) separated by ridges (*clints*). The grykes and clints are a result of the chemical weathering of natural cracks or joints in the limestone.

Other features of limestone weathering and erosion are shown in the model of a limestone landscape in Figure A.

Underground water and the hydrological cycle

Although only 0.6 per cent of the earth's water is in underground aquifers, this is six times more than there is in lakes and rivers. Underground water becomes an important source of water supply where surface water is scarce or absent. In Australia only the eastern portion of the continent has all-year rivers (Figure B). In most of the rest of the continent, water supply and settlement depend on underground water. Fortunately artesian basins underlie 1.3 million square kilometres of Australia. The water is saline and can only be used for watering livestock. Without it, however, the interior of Australia would have attracted even fewer people than it has today.

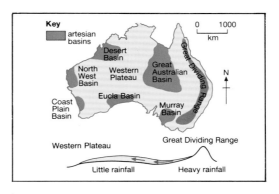

Figure B Artesian basins in Australia

QUESTIONS

1 Use an atlas to locate and name an area of Britain where you would expect to find:
   a) mountain limestone
   b) an artesian basin
   c) a chalk escarpment

2 Explain why:
   a) there is little surface drainage on chalk or limestone
   b) bare limestone surfaces are often found carved with deep cracks

3 Find *two* examples to show how settlement can sometimes be dependent on underground water.

4 Study Figure C, which shows the drainage system of the upper Aire in North Yorkshire.
   a) Explain why the stream draining Malham Tarn southwards comes to an end at **W**.
   b) Name the features shown at **V** and **W**. How does the stream form these features?
   c) Experiments with coloured water have shown that the water from stream **V** emerges from Malham Cove at **X**, while water from stream **W** reappears at Airehead Springs (**Y**). What happens to the two streams underground? Explain how this can occur.
   d) What features might you expect to find underground between **V** and **X**?

5 Find out where your own water supply comes from. Where are your local reservoirs? Where does their water come from? Are they dependent on underground water?

Fieldwork
Fieldwork to observe underground features in limestone is very dangerous. *Never* attempt it unless you have been given approval to join a party of *specialist potholers*.

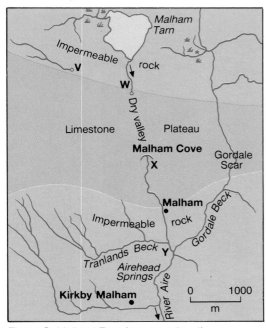

Figure C Malham Tarn (see question 4)

Unit 4 ASSESSMENT

The block diagram (Figure A) shows the catchment of an imaginary river, the Ripple. The catchment area is very heavily forested. The main town of the area, Ripplehampton, stands on either side of the Ripple. In winter and early spring the Ripple has a very heavy flow, and in recent years it has burst its banks and flooded the town several times.

The town council have heard that the Forestry Commission intends to cut down most of the timber in the catchment area over the next few years. It will be several years more before replanting can take place. The borough surveyor has informed the council that deforestation might be a problem for the town by increasing the likelihood of flooding. The council has appointed you as a hydrologist to study the problem further.

Work through the following tasks. By so doing you will be able to give the town council more detailed information about the problem, and perhaps offer some advice.

1 Why is the Figure A described as a 'cycle'? (3 marks)

2 Match up the list of terms below with the letters **P**, **Q**, **R** and **S** on Figure A:

precipitation	**P** = ...
evaporation	**Q** = ...
interception	**R** = ...
ground water flow	**S** = ...
surface runoff	(4 marks)

3 Explain what is meant by:
a) transpiration
b) throughflow (2 marks)

4 Study the table on the right.

a) Produce a hydrograph to show this data. On the graph label the times of peak discharge and rainfall. (8 marks)

b) Suggest why there is a difference in time between the two peaks. (2 marks)

Figure A The catchment of the River Ripple

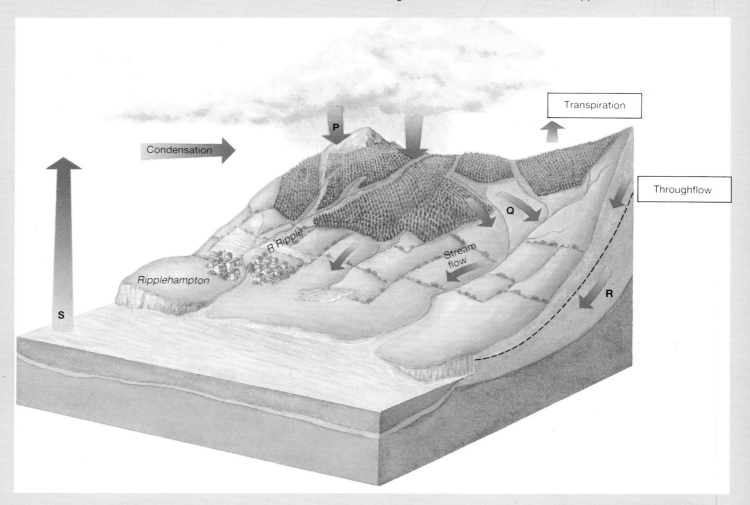

Rainfall and river discharge at Ripplehampton after a heavy storm

Number of hours after start of storm	Rainfall (mm)	Discharge (cumecs)
1	2	0.21
2	10	0.21
3	16	0.21
4	14	0.20
5	10	0.20
6	—	0.47
7	—	0.73
8	—	1.0
9	—	1.0
10	—	0.85
11	—	0.70
12	—	0.65
13	—	0.45
14	—	0.30
15	—	0.25
16	—	0.20

c) The river channel through Ripplehampton can cope with 0.80 cumecs before the river overspills its banks. Show this limit on the graph. For how many hours would the river have been flooding during this storm?   (3 marks)

5 Describe how you think deforestation of the catchment area would be likely to affect the following:

a) the amount of interception   (2 marks)

b) the amount of surface runoff   (2 marks)

c) the amount of moisture transpired   (2 marks)

d) the amount of water in the Ripple   (2 marks)

e) the response of the catchment to storms   (2 marks)

f) the flood situation in the town following heavy storms.   (2 marks)

6 Some people have put forward the following suggestions for coping with the problem:

● build a reservoir up the valley to store floodwaters

● rebuild the town on higher ground

● construct a new, straighter, broader, river channel through the town

● make the Forestry Commission plant even more trees in the catchment

● create washlands in suitable areas

a) Rearrange this list in rank order of your preference   (4 marks)

b) In a report justify the scheme you prefer   (12 marks)

Total: 50 marks

Details for pupil profile sheets Unit 4

Knowledge and understanding

1 The hydrological cycle as a system. The elements of the cycle

2 Processes at work within the hydrological cycle

3 Features formed by water underground

4 World water resources

5 The hydrological cycle and human activities – water supply, settlement, the flood hazard

Skills

1 Construction and interpretation of hydrographs under varying hydrological conditions

2 Making field measurements – transpiration, infiltration

3 Decision-making using hydrological data

Values

1 Awareness of the role of water as a human resource

2 Awareness of varying human responses to the flood hazard

Unit 5: Down the river

River regimes

Figure A shows some of the different river *regimes* around the world. A river's regime is a fingerprint of the factors which control the flow of water in the *catchment*. The catchment or *drainage basin* is the area from which all the river's water comes from. The boundary of a catchment area is called a *watershed*. Within the watershed, any water that runs off the land's surface eventually finds its way into the river through streams and *tributaries*. Further water is stored in lakes, swamps and rocks. *Streamflow* or *discharge* describes the amount of water flowing in a river. Rainfall and discharge are closely linked.

A river's flow pattern is very important for people who live close to the river and gain their livelihoods from it – especially by fishing or by irrigated agriculture. People can also manage or control a river's flow for their own use – by constructing dams for irrigation, flood control, and electricity generation.

Figure A World river regimes and climates (adapted from the *Geographical Magazine*)

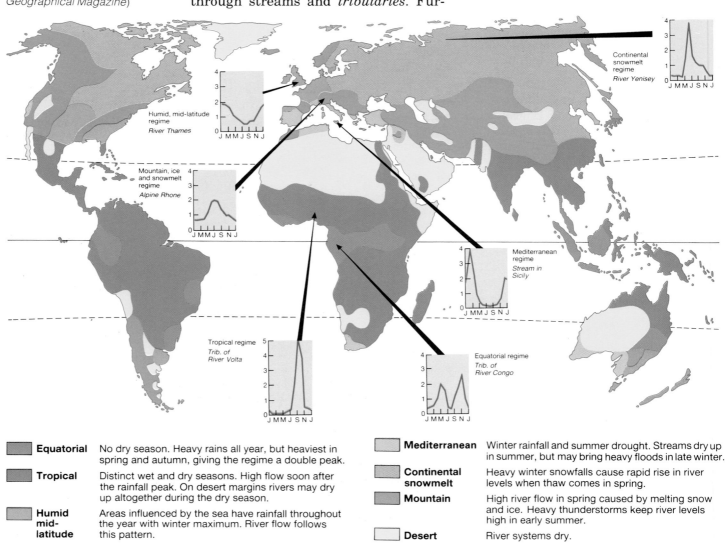

	Equatorial	No dry season. Heavy rains all year, but heaviest in spring and autumn, giving the regime a double peak.
	Tropical	Distinct wet and dry seasons. High flow soon after the rainfall peak. On desert margins rivers may dry up altogether during the dry season.
	Humid mid-latitude	Areas influenced by the sea have rainfall throughout the year with winter maximum. River flow follows this pattern.
	Mediterranean	Winter rainfall and summer drought. Streams dry up in summer, but may bring heavy floods in late winter.
	Continental snowmelt	Heavy winter snowfalls cause rapid rise in river levels when thaw comes in spring.
	Mountain	High river flow in spring caused by melting snow and ice. Heavy thunderstorms keep river levels high in early summer.
	Desert	River systems dry.

The Niger

The Niger (Figures B and C) in West Africa is the world's seventh longest river. In the upper Niger basin discharge is very low during the long dry season. While the dry Harmattan wind blows from the Sahara desert, riverflow depends on the slow release of stored groundwater.

July brings wet winds from the southwest. Water quickly runs off the bare rock surfaces of this semi-desert region. For a few weeks discharge is very high. This ends very quickly when the wet season is over.

In the lower Niger basin wet onshore winds dominate most of the year. The regime is more even, and the discharge peak is much less pronounced.

Figure B The catchment of the Niger showing rainfall and discharge at Baro in the wet season

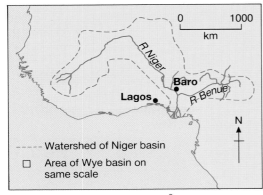

Area of Niger basin 1 112 000 km²
Length of Niger 4080 km

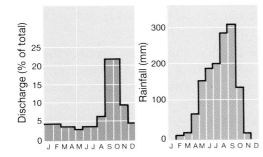

Figure C The confluence of the River Niger and the River Benue

The Wye

The River Wye is one of Britain's major rivers. The Wye's regime closely reflects the pattern of rainfall in the basin (Figure D). On the steep hillslopes of mid-Wales, water quickly runs downslope into stream channels. Although some moisture takes a longer route by infiltration and throughflow, river volume responds fairly quickly to changes in precipitation.

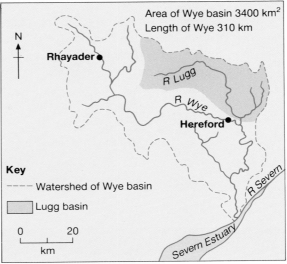

Figure D The catchment of the River Wye showing rainfall and discharge at Rhayader in the upper Wye basin

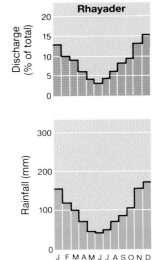

QUESTIONS

1 Write down:
   a) the rainfall at Rhayader in February
   b) the percentage of the Wye's streamflow that is discharged at Rhayader during February
   c) the rainfall at Baro in September
   d) the percentage of the Niger's streamflow discharged at Baro during September
   e) the month when discharge at Baro is at its lowest
   f) the month when discharge at Rhayader is at its peak.

2 Give a reason why:
   a) there is little rain at Baro in March
   b) peak discharge at Baro lags behind peak rainfall
   c) the discharge pattern at Rhayader closely follows the rainfall pattern.

3 Look at Figure A. Find:
   a) another river with a regime similar to the Wye
   b) another river with a regime similar to the Niger
   c) an area of the world which has two rainfall peaks per year
   d) an area of the world where snowmelt influences river regimes

4 Why do people need to know about river regimes?

Figures A and B shows a group of students studying a stream in Gwynedd, north Wales. In Gwynedd the mountains reach to the coast, so that many streams are quite short in length.

Figure A Students at Site B on Afon Hen

Figure B Students use a watch, a metre rule and a float to measure the velocity of Afon Hen

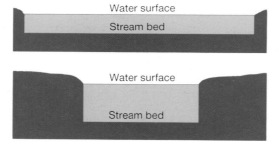

Figure C Cross-sections of two stream channels

The stream studied by the students, the Afon Hen, is shown on the Ordnance Survey map extract on page 126. Use the map extract to answer question 1 before you continue reading.

The students worked on the stream at points **P**, **Q** and **R**, shown by arrows on the map. They decided to test the hypothesis that the stream would move more quickly downstream at **R** than it would at **P** or **Q**. Their reasons for this were:

• the gradient was less at **R** than at **P** or **Q**.

• the stream probably carried more sediment downstream and therefore moved more slowly.

Testing the hypothesis

By measuring the time it took for an object to float a measured distance down the stream, the students calculated the stream's velocity at points **P**, **Q** and **R**. Their results are shown in the table below. Do these results prove the hypothesis?

Stream velocity (metres per second) at sites on Afon Hen

Site P	Site Q	Site R
0.55	0.61	0.80

According to the table, the stream flows *faster* at point **R** than it does at **P** or **Q**. The reasons for this are:

• Close to the stream's source the *channel* is full of jagged pebbles and boulders. The water slows down as it swirls round them.

• Further downstream, sediments deposited by the stream smooth out the channel bed. There is less friction so the water moves faster.

• The deeper channel downstream allows a smoother, faster flow of water (Figure D).

The stream at work

The student party looked into how the Afon Hen *erodes* its bed and banks and gathers a *load* of eroded material. Some of the erosion processes are described in the panel on the right.

As the Afon Hen swirls pebbles and sand grains against each other, the rough edges are gradually worn away and the particles become more rounded. At each of the three sites the students carried out some measurements on samples of pebbles to work out their *roundness index*. In this index highly rounded pebbles produce high values. The table below shows the results.

Roundness index of pebbles from three sites along Afon Hen

Sample 1	Sample 2	Sample 3
560	300	370

Unfortunately the students forgot to write down from which of the three sites (**P**, **Q**, or **R**) each sample came. Can you help them to work out the site to which each sample belongs?

Figure D How to make a simple sampling bottle

direction of river flow
rod
retort stand clamp
bent glass tube
milk bottle
straight glass tube

How a river erodes

Hydraulic action The water swirls out loose pebbles and particles from around the channelbed and sides

Corrasion Pebbles, stones, and sediment scour and wear away the channel bed and sides

Abrasion Pebbles and stones rub against each other in the stream and are worn down in size

Solution Soluble rock material – especially calcium carbonate in chalk or limestone – is dissolved by the slightly acidic stream water

QUESTIONS

1 From the map extract on page 126, make a tracing of the coastline and stream.
   a) Use the straight edge of a piece of paper to measure the length of the Afon Hen from your traced map.
   b) On your map draw a line to enclose all points within which any water is likely to drain into the Afon Hen or its tributaries. Colour the area inside the line, and label the catchment area and watershed.
   c) Write a sentence about the factors that made you decide where to draw the line representing the watershed.

2 Explain to a friend how you would use the stopwatch, metre rule, and a stream float (see Figure B) to measure stream velocity.

3 Copy and complete the following table:

Features of the Afon Hen

Feature	Site P	Site Q	Site R
Gradient	steep		
Velocity (m/s)		0.61	
Friction			
Roughness of channel	many pebbles and boulders		
Shape of channel			
Roundness of particles			

4 The two cross-sections in Figure C have the same area. Measure the length of bed and banks in contact with the water in each case. In which sort of channel is the stream most likely to be slowed down by friction with the bed and banks?

5 **Fieldwork**
   a) Make a simple sampling bottle like the one shown in Figure D.
   b) Take a sample of water from a river. Weigh a piece of filter paper. Strain the sample through a funnel containing the filter paper. Let the filter paper dry and then weigh it. Subtract the weight of the filter paper. You have now worked out the weight of the sediment (suspended load) in the sample.
   c) Measure the rate of flow of the river.
   d) Repeat the sampling at different points along the river's course or from the same point at different times. Use the results to see if the suspended load varies with the rate of flow.

5.3
Down the valley

Figure A The headwaters of the Ribble

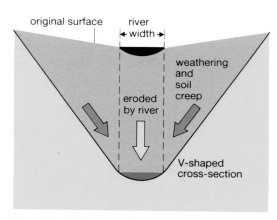

Figure B (*left*) Downcutting

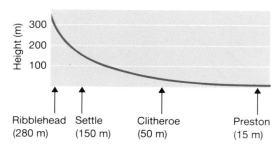

Figure C The long profile

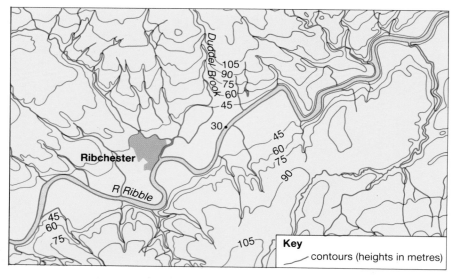

Figure D The flood plain of the Ribble near Clitheroe

Figure E Meander features

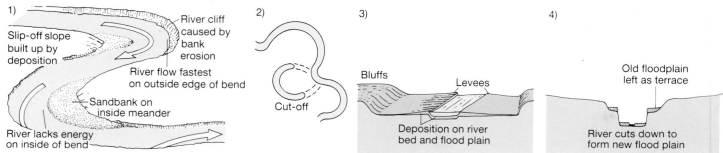

Near the source

Figure A shows the Pennines near Ribblehead in North Yorkshire. This is the *headwater zone* of the River Ribble. Tributaries of the Ribble in this area and are close to the Ribble's watershed with its neighbouring drainage basins.

Rapid downcutting in the headwater zone (Figure B) is one way in which the river tries to achieve a state of balance. As the river cuts down further, so the surface of the land is lowered. This in turn reduces the gradient. With a gentler gradient, less energy is used for downcutting. Gradient, energy, and downcutting are closely interrelated.

The long profile

Further downstream the Ribble's gradient is much gentler, so that from source to mouth the river has a concave *long profile* (Figure C). The long profile of the Ribble is mostly smooth, but in many rivers irregularities in the profile can be picked out. The main sorts of irregularities in a river's long profile are waterfalls, rapids and lakes.

Meanders

Figure D shows the Ribble much further from its source, about 20 km from the sea. It shows the Ribble beginning to meander.

Meanders often occur where a river flows with a gentle gradient. Along the lower parts of valleys heavy flow gives

48

Figure F The Cuckmere River in Sussex

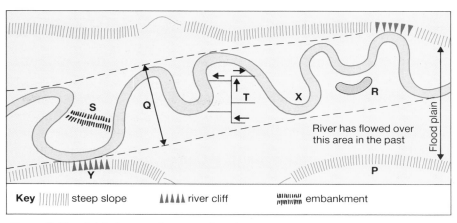

Key ||||||| steep slope   ▲▲▲▲▲ river cliff   embankment

Figure G Floodplain features (see question 5)

the river a lot of spare energy. The gentle gradient means that it cannot use this energy on downcutting. It uses it instead to lengthen its course by developing meanders (Figure E).

Meanders do not stay in the same place. Undercutting of river cliffs makes meanders wider. Gravity also causes meander belts to 'migrate' gradually downstream.

Alluvial floodplains

The meander belt of the Ribble forms part of its *floodplain*. The floodplain is the area which could be flooded if the river bursts its banks. The floodplain is covered with sediment or *alluvium* deposited by the river. With repeated deposition the river channel may even be built up above the height of the flood plain. Natural *levees* or embankments (Figure E) are the only things that then protect the flood plain from flooding.

Many rivers now flood much less than in the past. Sometimes this is because the headwaters have been tapped for water supply or irrigation, reducing the river's discharge. In other cases flooding has been reduced by cutting a new, straighter, deeper channel which can carry more water away quicker. The old channel is then abandoned.

In many parts of the world flooding by rivers is not always seen as a problem. The floodplains and deltas of rivers such as the Mekong or Nile are densely populated. People rely on the regular annual flooding of the rivers to spread fertile silt and natural irrigation water across their fields.

QUESTIONS

1 a) Trace the map of the Ribble (Figure D), roughly marking in the 45 m, 60 m and 75 m contour lines.
   b) Shade the area of flat land bordering the river. Mark with dark shading those places where the river is bordered by steeply rising land.
   c) Using Figure E to help you, label the following:
      meanders   flood plain
      bluffs   meander belt

2 Name and describe:
   a) *three* features which characterise the headwater zone of a river
   b) *three* features which are typical of the lower course of a river
   c) *two* features which might cause irregularities in a river's long profile.

3 Along the lower course of a river, what features would you look for to show that:
   a) despite the gentler gradient, the river is still eroding
   b) the river flows more slowly on the insides of bends
   c) the river once followed a different course

4 What features of a river would you look for to show that:
   a) irregularities are 'temporary' features of a river's life
   b) people often find flooding inconvenient
   c) alluvial features change in position
   d) gradient determines how the river uses its energy

5 Study Figure G which shows some floodplain features
   a) Name the features shown at **P**, **Q**, and **R**
   b) Describe the processes and changes which are taking place at **X**, and **Y**
   c) Expain why there are no settlements shown on this map
   d) Suggest what the features marked **S** and **T** might be used for
   e) Further upstream the river has been dammed to make a reservoir for water supply. What effect will this have on the features shown in this map?

Fieldwork

6 Find a stretch of a river with well developed meanders. From a suitable viewpoint sketch and label the features of the meanders. Add further labels to illustrate the processes which are occurring.

5.4 Drainage patterns

Figure A shows some different patterns of drainage. They readily develop on surfaces where there is only one rock type. But they also occur on surfaces where there are rocks of different hardness. In some way the streams develop a pattern which is not influenced by the rock structure. Dendritic patterns can be created by chance. Perhaps this is why they are so common in the natural world. Try question 1 before you carry on reading.

Squares and spokes

Figure C shows an area of the Appalachian mountains in eastern North America. Here some streams have eroded along the ridges of anticlines where the rocks are weak through being 'stretched' (see page 15). Tributaries have developed at right angles to the main rivers, parallel to the gradient of the slopes. These processes give the drainage pattern a squarish or *trellis* appearance.

Figure D shows Dartmoor in southwestern England. Dartmoor is a *batholith*, or large intruded mass of granite. Streams have developed running off Dartmoor in a *radial* pattern, rather like the spokes of a wheel. They often have steep gradients where they cross the edge of the granite on to the lower surrounding countryside.

Figure A Drainage patterns

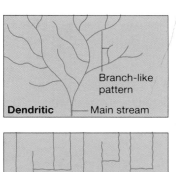

Dendritic — Branch-like pattern — Main stream

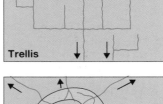

Trellis

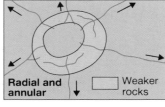

Radial and annular — Weaker rocks

Figure B The random drainage pattern exercise (see exercise 1)

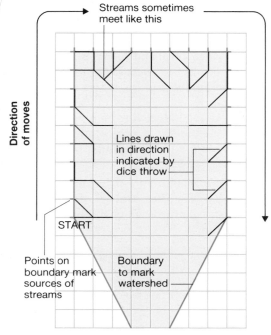

Streams sometimes meet like this

Direction of moves

Lines drawn in direction indicated by dice throw

START

Points on boundary mark sources of streams

Boundary to mark watershed

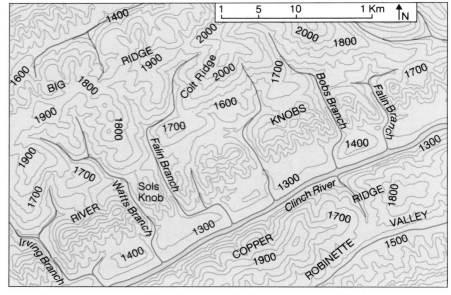

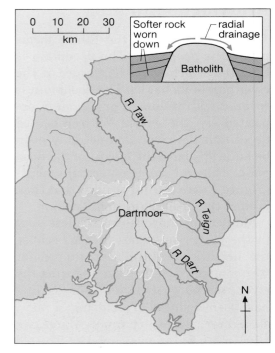

Figure D (*above*) Radial drainage off Dartmoor (inset shows the batholith formation that causes radial drainage)

Softer rock worn down — radial drainage — Batholith

R Taw

Dartmoor

R Teign

R Dart

Figure C (*left*) Trellis drainage in the Appalachian Mountains, USA

Inland drainage

In dry or arid areas, rain occurs so infrequently that any streams dry up long before they reach the sea. There is little opportunity for any stream networks or drainage patterns to develop. An atlas map of Australia will show you that most of this continent has no permanent stream networks. Most of the permanent rivers are in the east, along the Great Dividing Range, and in the south-west (see page 31). Rivers in the north are highly seasonal and depend upon the monsoon rains. Elsewhere there are no rain-bearing winds to sustain permanent streamflow.

In arid areas where faulting has produced enclosed basins or depressions, inland drainage patterns may develop. Occasional storms produce temporary streams which drain together into an inland or *playa* lake. These lakes quickly evaporate, leaving behind dissolved salts. Over thousands of years evaporation has built up hundreds of metres of thickness of salts on the lake floors.

Lake Eyre in South Australia is one of the world's largest playa lakes. Its drainage basin extends over most of central Australia. Most of the time it is dry, its bed consisting entirely of a salt crust. In 1950–1, after a period of exceptionally heavy rain, it grew into a shallow sheet of water 5000 sq km in extent. By 1953 however it had mostly dried out and dwindled once again to an area of salt-pans.

Figure E The Etosha Pan, an inland drainage basin in Namibia in south-western Africa

Figure F Lake Eyre, a playa lake in South Australia

QUESTIONS

1 a) Take a sheet of A4 graph paper and mark it out as shown in red on Figure B. The points around the edge are the 'starting points' for headwater streams.
b) Throw a die to get a random pattern of 'moves'. The moves are:
1 = west, 2 = south-west, 3 = south, 4 = south-east, 5 = east,
6 = throw again. A six-sided pencil can be used for this. Move one square for each throw.
c) Work clockwise around the watershed, creating new stream movements in rotation. When you have been round once, start again, adding to each stream in turn.
d) What happens to the stream pattern? Is it easy to form a dendritic pattern? Is your 'game' a fair reflection of how stream patterns develop in reality?

2 Name a region where you would expect to find an example of:
a) trellis drainage
b) radial drainage
c) a salt lake

3 Describe *two* conditions likely to give rise to inland drainage basins

4 a) Decide which of the following statements are *true* and which are *false*.
    i) Much of Australia is without river networks
    ii) Dartmoor was once a volcano
    iii) Rock structures hardly ever influence drainage patterns
    iv) In the Appalachians many rivers follow anticlinal ridges
    v) Playa lakes are caused by the deposition of salts
    vi) Drainage density mostly varies according to precipitation
    vii) Bare rock surfaces give rise to little drainage
b) Give *correct* versions of the false statements you have picked out.

The Colorado River is the longest river (2320 km) in the USA and drains 8 per cent of that country. It is one of the world's most disputed rivers, since its water is shared between seven North American states and also with Mexico. Figure A shows how some of the water is used. So much water is taken from the Colorado that only a trickle reaches the sea.

Figure A Use of the Colorado River

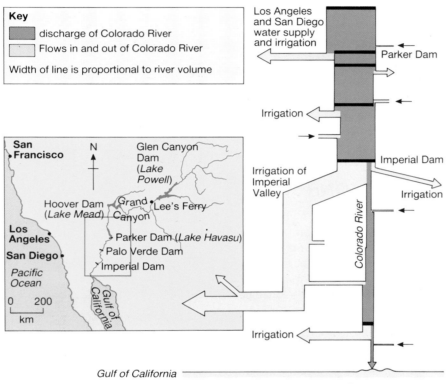

Where it starts

The Colorado rises in the Rocky Mountains of Wyoming, Colorado, and New Mexico. In this region the river has a high spring and summer discharge because of the effects of melting snow and high runoff from thunderstorms.

Further downriver, the Colorado passes through the spectacular Grand Canyon (Figure B), in places 24 km wide and 1500 m deep. The river drops 655 m from Lee's Ferry through the Canyon to Lake Mead, passing through 161 sets of rapids. Through the Canyon, the river once had an average discharge of 2264 cumecs which rose to over 3400 cumecs in times of flood. This huge flood could move 140 million tonnes of sediment through the Canyon in some years. In one day alone in 1927, it carried 27.6 million tonnes – the equivalent of 900000 fully loaded trucks.

Massive discharges like this can make a lot of difference to the Colorado's cross-profile. Figure C shows how the cross-profile changed during a period of several days of heavy flooding in 1956. Some of the Colorado's terraces in the Grand Canyon can be related to the levels the river used to reach during high discharges.

Figure B The Colorado River passing through a stretch of the Grand Canyon

A river made into lakes

The Colorado has been dammed at several points to generate hydroelectricity and to provide irrigation water for in-

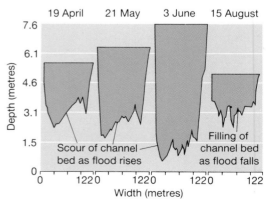

Figure C Changes in the Colorado's cross profile during floods

tensive agriculture. The first of these dams was the Hoover Dam, completed in 1935, creating Lake Mead behind it. Lake Mead is 184 km long and can store the equivalent of two years flow of the river. The dam is used for hydroelectricity, flood control, and irrigation. Figure A shows some of the other dams on the Colorado.

Controlling the river in this way has brought about some important changes to the river itself. One example is the Glen Canyon Dam. The panel below shows some of the effects downstream.

Impact downstream of the Glen Canyon Dam

- Reduced river flow
- Sediment concentration fell by 200 per cent
- Flood peaks smoothed out and now depend much more on when electricity is wanted, such as peak times on weekdays
- Alluvial terraces once covered by the river much of the time have been eroded by the wind
- Freshwater fish suited to habitats with turbulent water have been replaced by those preferring clearer waters, such as trout.

Above the dam, Lake Powell is gradually becoming infilled with sediment from the river basin upstream.

Tamed rivers worldwide

Hardly any of the world's major rivers now remain in their natural state. Most have been changed by people to some degree (Figure D). Over the last century dams and reservoirs have not only become more numerous but have been getting bigger. At present, 500 new dams are built around the world every year. By the end of the century more than 60 per cent of the world's total stream flow will be regulated by people in some way.

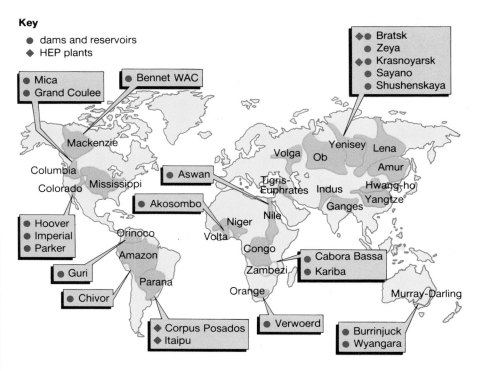

Key
- ● dams and reservoirs
- ◆ HEP plants

Figure D The world's main river basins. All the world's largest rivers are now controlled by man in some way

---

QUESTIONS

1 With the help of an atlas, name which states the Colorado River passes through.

2 Name *four* points at which the Colorado is dammed for human use.

3 Describe:
  a) *two* factors which control the Colorado's pattern of discharge in its upper basin
  b) *two* factors which control its discharge pattern in its lower basin
  c) *two* ways in which its discharge pattern has been modifying its channel form.

4 Study Figure C which shows how part of the Colorado's channel changed during a heavy flood.
  a) About how long did the flood last?
  b) Between April 19 and June 3 how much higher did the river become?
  c) Between June 3 and August 15 how much infill occurred?
  d) A few years later the Glen Canyon Dam was built upstream. How would it have affected the pattern in this diagram?

5 Imagine you had to produce a film about how the Colorado has been changing. What sorts of changes would you include? Which sorts of changes would most interest the public?

6 'Even in remote areas river basins are being changed by people.' List some evidence for this view.

5.6 River's end

Estuaries are not only the ends of rivers. They are a sort of crossroads where land, river and sea all meet. Figure A shows how these physical systems mix and influence each other. Notice how:

● There is an outgoing *river flow* and also a *tidal flow* (made up of a *flood tide*, coming in, and *ebb tide*, going out).

● The *shape* of the estuary helps to control the river flow. Rivers flowing into straight estuaries will have more spare energy than those flowing into funnel shaped ones. Rivers can scour straight estuaries and keep them free from sediment.

● Estuaries have greater *tidal ranges* than the open sea. Tidal range is the difference in height between high and low tides. The shape of the estuary increases the tidal range by 'piling up' the incoming water.

● *Sediment* in the estuary comes from downwashing by the river, and is also brought inshore by sea currents.

Estuaries are the dumping grounds for everything the river carries. This includes not only sediment and dissolved rock material, but also the waste products (such as sewage and industrial effluents) of the towns, cities and industries along the river's banks. Even the chemicals used in fertilisers get washed into the river and down to its estuary.

The Mississippi Delta

The satellite image (Figure B) shows the delta of the River Mississippi in the Gulf of Mexico. A delta is a level plain almost at sea level formed by deposition at the river's mouth. The delta of the Mississippi is one of the world's largest. It covers 26 000 square kilometres, an area almost the size of Belgium. Each year the river dumps 450 million tons of sediment into the delta and the Gulf of Mexico beyond it.

As the Mississippi river reaches its mouth, its velocity and energy is slowed by contact with the sea currents. It drops its coarser sediment first, forming a bar a few metres below water level. The finer river silt is carried out into the sea, where it builds up as a series of sloping layers. At first the finest clays are slow to settle, but the salt water makes the particles join together and finally sink. On the satellite image the sediment carried out to sea appears as a light blue 'cloud'.

The Mississippi delta is constantly changing. Figure C shows some of the processes that are at work all the time.

New Orleans

New Orleans is one of America's major cities, with a population of more than a

Figure A An estuary, the meeting point of several physical systems

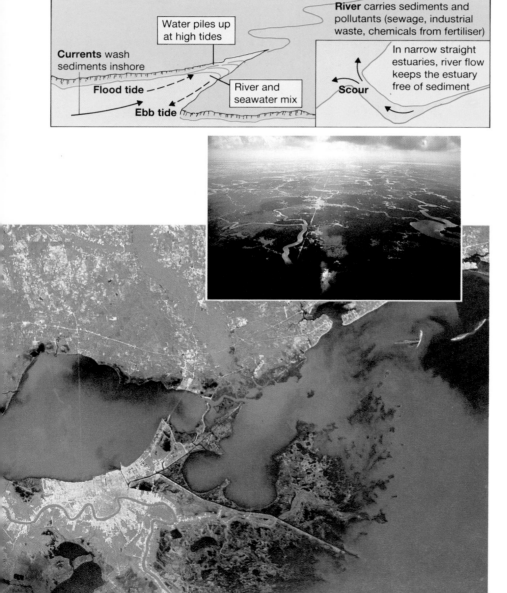

Figure B Satellite and aerial (*inset*) images of the Mississippi Delta

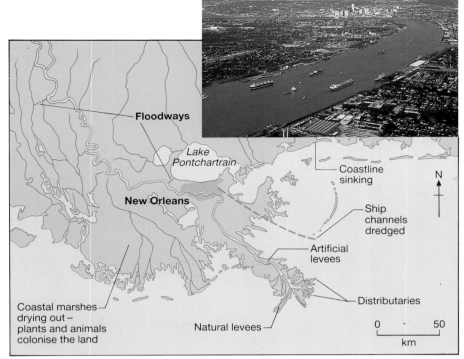

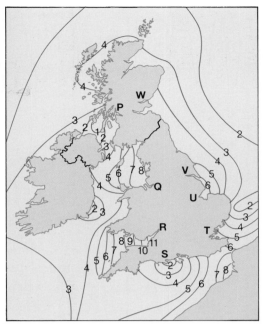

Figure C Processes at work continually in the Mississippi Delta and (*inset*) New Orleans, a delta city

Figure D Tidal ranges (measured in Metres) and estuaries around Britain (see question 3)

million people. It is entirely a 'delta city' and is protected from the Mississippi floods by levees on all sides.

These levees can also be a problem because they can prevent rainwater from draining away. There were disastrous floods in 1927 which left 700 000 people homeless. In 1935 a floodway was created north of the city, so that floodwaters could escape directly into Lake Pontchartrain and then into the Gulf of Mexico. Since then further measures have been taken to prevent flooding: a second floodway has been created and dredging of the existing channels goes on all the time. Dredging also keeps the channels free of sediment for navigation; the Mississippi is one of America's major waterways.

Many of the world's cities are located on estuaries. Heavy industries such as oil refining and power generation are often found on estuaries. Estuaries and deltas are the homes to many millions of people who depend on the annual floodwaters for their crops and livelihoods. However, estuaries are also habitats for much rare wildlife. All this means that there are many demands made on estuarine environments.

QUESTIONS

1 Give the term used for:
 a) the difference in height between high and low tide
 b) a river channel formed from the division of a larger channel mud banks along the river's edge.

2 Describe *three* ways in which human activity makes demands on estuaries.

3 Study Figure E which shows tidal range around Britain
 a) Name the estuaries **P–W**.
 b) identify *two* estuaries which ought to be suitable for tidal barrages that could be used to generate electricity. State why you think they are suitable.
 c) Suggest the effect that the construction of tidal barrages might have on the following:
  i) the movement of sediment up and down the estuaries
  ii) water and shore wildlife behind the barrage
  iii) opportunities for transport developments
  iv) opportunities for leisure developments.

4 Using the satellite image of the Mississippi delta (Figure B)
 a) Make a tracing or copy to show the outline of the delta and the main channels. Use colouring to shade in the farmed areas, flooded areas and offshore sediment.
 b) Suggest *three* ways in which satellite images can provide information which might not be found on a map or aerial photograph.

5 Explain:
 a) how new land is being formed at the Mississippi delta;
 b) how New Orleans is kept free of the flood hazard.

6 'Estuaries are important to people in many ways.' Find some information to support this idea.

Figure A The Upper Barle valley, Exmoor, Somerset

Figure B The Wye valley near Chepstow, Gwent

For this assessment unit refer to the rivers in Figures A, B and C
>   River A: the Upper Barle
>   River B: the Wye
>   River C: the Teign

1 Which of the three rivers:
   a) has the widest channel?
   b) has the straightest channel?
   c) has the steepest gradient?
   d) has the steepest valley sides?   (4 marks)

2 What evidence do the photographs provide of the following:
   a) the valley of River A has not been interfered with much by people
   b) the valley of River B supports more human use than the valley of River A
   c) people are very dependent on the estuary of River C.   (6 marks)

3 Draw a sketch cross-section across River B (Figure B). On your cross-section label the following features:
   a) a *slip-off slope*
   b) a *river cliff*
   c) the direction of *meander* shift
   d) a point of high river energy and velocity
   e) a point of low river energy and velocity
   f) a possible former edge of the meander belt. (12 marks)

4 Using tracing paper make an overlay of the main features of River C (Figure C).
   a) On your tracing show:
      i) the direction of river movement
      ii) the position of sandbanks
      iii) areas of urban development
   b) Beneath the tracing:
      i) name *two* physical systems which are illustrated
      ii) list *three* ways in which sediment may be moved by water in the areas shown
      iii) list ways in which people may be altering the environment of the estuary.   (12 marks)

5 Produce a sketch of the landscape shown in Figure A. On your sketch add the following labels at appropriate points:
   Heavy surface runoff
   Downcutting is stronger than valley widening
   Bedload deposited at low discharge
   Meanders developing
   Rounding of plateau edges by weathering   (10 marks)

Figure C The Teign estuary, Teignmouth, Devon

6 Outline how you would collect field data to measure the
following:
a) the velocity of the River Barle
b) the roundness of pebbles from the River Wye
c) Sediment concentration in the lower Teign (6 marks)

7 Describe how the types of data collected in question 6 can
be used to show that:
a) river velocity usually increases from source to mouth
b) pebble roundness usually increases downstream
(6 marks)

8 a) Explain what is meant by the term *runoff regime*
b) Describe the main features of the runoff regime of the
River Wye (see page 44).
c) Would you expect the regimes of the Teign and Barle
to be different from or similar to the regime of the Wye?
Give reasons. (9 marks)

9 Imagine there is a project to dam the upland tract of the
Barle and convert it into a reservoir to supply water to a
nearby town. What impact would the dam have further
downstream on:
a) the river's regime?
b) the river's capacity to transport sediment?
c) peaks and troughs in the river's flow pattern?
(10 marks)
Total: 75 marks

Details for pupil profile sheets Unit 5

Knowledge and understanding

1 Location of the world's main rivers and basins
2 Features of drainage basins; patterns, density
3 River regimes – the controlling factors; world
patterns
4 Channel features and processes
5 Long profile features and processes – including
headwater, meander, and floodplain features
6 Effects of human interference with river flow
7 Features of estuaries and deltas
8 Potential and problems of estuaries and deltas for
human use

Skills

1 Construction of river regime graphs
2 Interpretation of drainage patterns from OS maps
3 Collection of data from fieldwork for river velocity,
pebble roundness, sediment concentration
4 Field sketching of river features
5 Interpretation of estuary features from satellite
images

Values

1 Awareness of importance of river flow patterns to
human activity
2 Awareness of importance of deltaic and floodplain
sites for settlement and agriculture
3 Awareness of man's abilities to control and change
flow patterns
4 Awareness of human responses to the flood hazard

Unit 6: Snow and ice at work

One night in April 1912 the ocean liner, *Titanic*, hit an iceberg off the coast of Labrador. Since then there has been a regular patrol in this region to warn ships of iceberg movements.

Most of the Labrador icebergs originate from *glaciers* in Greenland (Figure A). The glaciers are part of the huge *ice-cap* which covers almost the whole of the continent. When the glaciers reach the deep inlets or *fiords* of the west coast, they spill out beyond the edge of the land into the frozen sea. In summer the sea thaws for a few weeks, so that the ice mass resting on it becomes unstable. Great blocks of ice break off and float away seawards as icebergs (Figure E). The Labrador Current moves the icebergs southwards into the main shipping lanes.

Images made by satellite 'sensing' are helping to monitor iceberg movements in the Labrador area. Figure C shows a LANDSAT satellite image of the Jakobshavns Isfiord in western Greenland. This is a long, narrow inlet of the sea. At the head of the fiord is a glacier called the Jakobshavns Isbrae. This is one of Greenland's biggest glaciers, carrying 11 per cent of the total ice discharge from the Greenland ice sheet.

You should easily be able to pick out the icebergs floating in the water. They have broken away from the ice cliff (6 km long and 70 m high) which forms the front edge of the glacier. The process of breaking away is called *calving*.

The image was taken in July 1982. It was one of 28 images of the fiord taken by the satellite between March and October as it orbited the earth. The images enabled the movements of individual icebergs to be monitored in detail. They showed that 25 major icebergs were calved in 1982. The icebergs remain drifting in the fiord for over a year before they are carried into the open sea.

How ice masses form

Ice masses form two per cent of all the water on the earth's surface. Most of this ice is in the ice-caps of Greenland and Antarctica. The remainder is in valley glaciers in high mountain areas such as the Alps, Pyrenees, Andes, or Himalayas.

In Greenland, ice masses build up readily because of the high latitude and low average temperatures; many mountain slopes lie above the permanent *snow-line* (Figure B). Over a period of months, fallen snow gradually becomes crushed and compacted under its own

Figure A (*below*) Origins and movements of icebergs in the Greenland area

Key

	main source of icebergs
	sea ice all year round
	sea ice in winter
→	iceberg tracks

0   500
km

Ellesmere Island
Hall Land
Baffin Bay
GREENLAND
Hudson Strait
Davis Strait
Jakobshavns Isfiord
Denmark Strait
Labrador
ICELAND
Icebergs drift towards shipping lanes

Figure B How ice caps form and spread

North facing slopes receive little heat from sun. Snow may remain all year round. Glaciers readily develop.

Precipitation as snow

South facing slopes Surface snow melted by warm sun in spring and summer. Not many glaciers.

Freshly fallen snow
Nevé or Firn
Glacier ice
moving outwards
Permanent snow line
Winter snow line
Valley glaciers
Sea
Mountain core
Crevasses (cracks in ice)

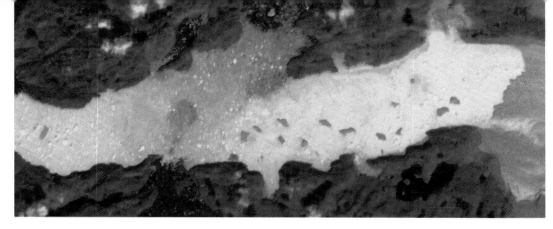

Figure C An image of the Jakobshavns Isfiord taken by the Landsat satellite on 28 July 1982

Figure D The main features of the Jakobshavn Isfiord

weight. On a warm spring day the surface layers melt and the water runs into the gaps between the crushed snowflakes. At night the mass re-freezes, becoming harder than before.

This process, repeated day after day, produces a brittle crystalline mass called *firn* or *névé*. After more compaction and refreezing (taking several years) all the air spaces are crushed out and the firn becomes solid ice.

In this way the highest parts of the Greenland mountains become centres of *ice dispersal*. These mountain cores became capped by the growing ice masses. Under the pressure of the growing *ice-caps* the ice is squeezed outwards. Tongues of solid ice are pushed down the slopes into the mountain valleys forming long *glaciers*. The glaciers eventually reach the coast at sea inlets like the Jakobshavns Isfiord.

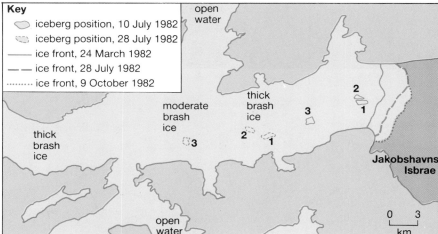

Key
- iceberg position, 10 July 1982
- iceberg position, 28 July 1982
- ice front, 24 March 1982
- ice front, 28 July 1982
- ice front, 9 October 1982

open water

thick brash ice

moderate brash ice

thick brash ice

Jakobshavns Isbrae

open water

0   3
km

Figure E Icebergs off the coast of Greenland

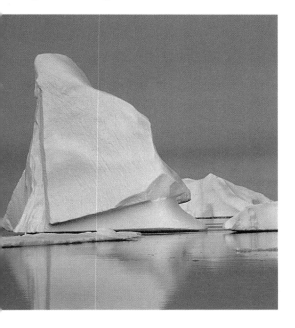

QUESTIONS

1 a) How far is an iceberg calved from Jakobshavns Isbrae likely to travel before it reaches the Atlantic shipping lanes?
   b) Why do icebergs drift along particular paths or tracks?

2 Why do you think there are so many winter sports resorts in the Alps and so few (or any) in Greenland?

3 Study the Landsat satellite image of Jakobshavns Isfiord taken on 28/7/82 (Figure C). Some of the main features of the image are shown in Figure D.
   a) Figure D shows the movement of the Jakobshavns Isbrae ice front between 24/3/82 and 9/10/82 as shown by Landsat images. How far did the ice retreat during this time?
   b) Figure D shows the movement of three large sample icebergs numbered 1, 2, 3 between 10/7/82 and 28/7/82. Find these three icebergs on the image.
   c) Calculate the average distance travelled by the three icebergs between these dates. What was the average rate of movement per day?
   d) Copy the outlines of Figure D. Draw your own 'image' of the Isfiord as it might appear in winter, showing the changes which will have taken place since the summer.

4 Suggest ways in which the following might find satellite images helpful:
   a) weather forecasters concerned with shipping
   b) operators of ski resorts

6.2 Glaciation: Cwm Idwal

Figure A (*Above*) View of Cwm Idwal

Cwm Idwal (Figure A) is a very scenic location with spectacular views. It is also an excellent example of a glaciated landscape. Over a hundred years ago scientists first used studies of the Idwal area to prove that parts of Britain had once been covered by ice sheets.

Using the landscape

A teacher took a student party to Cwm Idwal to study the area in detail. The first thing that they were going to look for was evidence of *glacial erosion*, that is, the work of ice in wearing down the landscape. Cwm Idwal's name is a good clue. A *cwm* (corrie, or cirque) is a major feature of a glaciated landscape. Figure A shows a handsheet issued to the students to explain how cwms are formed. The students made sketches (Figure C) of the features around them and recorded their observations. They were especially asked to think about the following questions:

● What are the typical features of a cwm or corrie?

● How many of these features appear in Cwm Idwal? Is Idwal a *good* example of a cwm?

● What glacial processes have formed the cwm?

● How are glaciated areas important to people?

Other glacial features

The students soon began to recognize other features typical of cwms and glacially eroded areas. At one end of the lake are huge slabs or boulders covered with long scratch marks called *striations*. These marks were made by the jagged stones carried along by the ice mass as it spilled out of the cwm. Some large boulders are smooth on the up-slope side and jagged on the downslope side. Some students explained these differences by referring to the processes

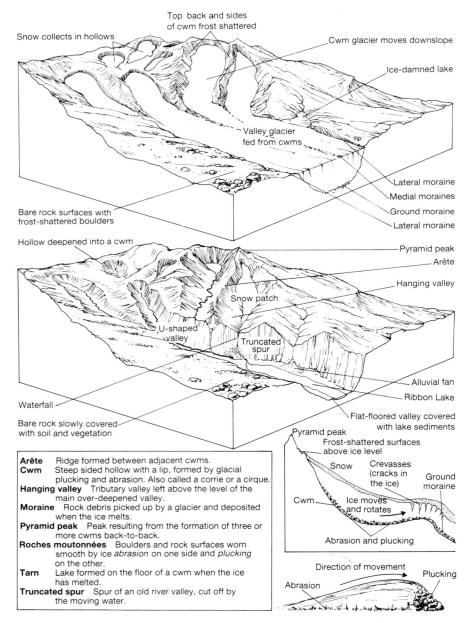

Figure B (*left*) Teacher's handsheet for students

Arête	Ridge formed between adjacent cwms.
Cwm	Steep sided hollow with a lip, formed by glacial plucking and abrasion. Also called a corrie or a cirque.
Hanging valley	Tributary valley left above the level of the main over-deepened valley.
Moraine	Rock debris picked up by a glacier and deposited when the ice melts.
Pyramid peak	Peak resulting from the formation of three or more cwms back-to-back.
Roches moutonnées	Boulders and rock surfaces worn smooth by ice *abrasion* on one side and *plucking* on the other.
Tarn	Lake formed on the floor of a cwm when the ice has melted.
Truncated spur	Spur of an old river valley, cut off by the moving water.

of *abrasion* and *plucking* described on the handsheet. They decided that the boulders were examples of the features called *roches moutonnées*. Other students noticed the hummocky mounds around the edge of the lake and wondered if they might be the remnants of the *moraines* carried by the ice.

The teacher then led the party to a point from where they could view and sketch the Nant Ffrancon pass (Figure D). She explained that the 'pass' is an example of a glaciated valley. It had once carried ice from Cwm Idwal and other cwms towards the North Wales coast.

How long ago?

The Ice Age which glaciated Cwm Idwal began about a million years ago but ended only about 10 000 years ago. Most of the Idwal features were formed just before the end of the glacial period. The Ice Age was not continuously cold but was made up of glacial periods separated by warmer periods (interglacials) when the ice melted altogether. Some scientists think that we are living in one of these interglacials and that the ice may come back. They have worked out that average annual temperatures would need to drop by only 1° C to bring glaciers back to places like Cwm Idwal.

Figure D The Nant Ffrancon pass

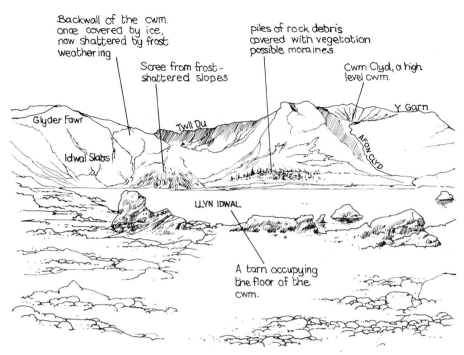

Figure C A student's sketch of Cwm Idwal

QUESTIONS

1 Describe the ways in which the area around Cwm Idwal is being used for:
   a) Leisure and tourism
   b) Education
   c) Farming

2 Describe the appearance of each of the following features, and explain how it has been formed:
   a) Truncated spur
   b) Hanging valley
   c) Arete

3 Produce a 'flow diagram' of boxes linked together by arrows. The words to put inside the boxes are as follows:

   rising temperatures·   ice masses grow
   cwms and glaciated valleys   lakes from meltwater
   falling temperatures   ice masses melt
   heavy snowfalls

   Make sure you put the boxes in the right order.

4 What evidence would you look for in a glaciated area to show that:
   a) you were standing in a cwm
   b) rock surfaces are scratched by the debris carried by moving ice
   c) the area had once been occupied by a lake formed from water from melting ice.

5 Assume that you were one of the students in the field party. Write a report on your findings at Cwm Idwal. Use the following headings:
   a) What we set out to do
   b) What we observed
   c) What we learned from our observations

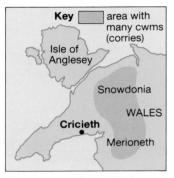

Figure A Location of Cricieth

Figure B Orientation of pebbles (*left*) and a sketch of the cliff face (*right*) at Cricieth

Figure B was drawn by a student on a field trip. It shows a coastal cliff at Cricieth in North Wales. The student thought it was important to record the following features about the cliff:
● It was made entirely of clay
● The clay contained many small pebbles.
● The clay was of two colours. The upper cliff was brown, the lower cliff blue-grey.

Patterns of ice movement

The cliff at Cricieth is made of *glacial till* or *boulder clay*. Figure C shows how till is carried along in the ice and eventually deposited. The Cricieth till contains pebbles and boulders which were too large to be worn down into clay. At Cricieth the till is easily recognizable because it forms a cliff.

Geographers use tills to help them work out the directions in which ice sheets moved. The pebbles in the ice swing round so that their long axes are parallel to the direction of ice movement – a sort of glacial 'streamlining'. The direction of orientation of pebbles exposed along a cliff like the Cricieth one can be measured (Figure B).

In Britain, northern Europe, and North America there are large areas of where till sheets form much of the relief, and provide the parent material of the soil. The clay soils derived from tills are the basis of much arable farming in the Midlands, East Anglia, eastern Denmark, and the American Mid-West.

Drumlins are hummocks or piles of till. They are formed from boulder clay deposited by ice and shaped while the ice was still moving. The end facing the ice source has a slightly steeper slope than the other end (Figure C).

Erratics (Figure D) are large boulders, often several feet high, which have been moved by the ice from their place of origin and transported on the ice surface, often many miles. The erratic was deposited only when the ice melted. Geologists can often match up an erratic with the parent rock outcrop

Figure C Features of glaciated landscapes, (*left*) at the ice front, (*right*) after the ice has melted

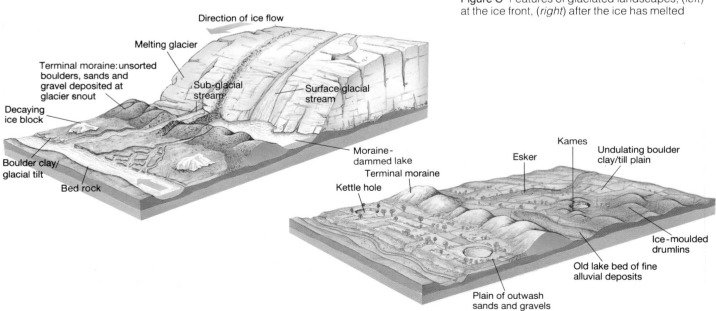

from which it was derived. This provides another way in which depositional features can tell us something about patterns of ice movement.

Melting ice

As glaciers and ice sheets continue to flow and spread, their edges or ice fronts move further and further from their source. Once the ice front reaches lowland plains, the lower temperatures may cause the ice front to begin to melt. The debris that is dumped along the melting ice front gradually grows into a huge pile or ridge. The ridge is called a *terminal moraine*. Geographers find terminal moraines useful because they show how far the ice advanced before it began to melt. They also show that the ice front must have been stationary for a long time. Further terminal moraines may mark standstill points.

Eventually rising temperatures in the ice source region prevent new ice formation. The entire ice mass then stagnates and quickly melts. Huge quantities of *meltwater* are formed. Some of this will remain ponded up between unmelted ice masses and hillsides, forming *meltwater lakes*.

Southern Finland

The map (Figure E) shows that much of Southern Finland consists of lakes. The lakes were formed at the end of the last glaciation when melting ice became trapped between mountains to the west and the ice front to the east. Deep lakes soon formed in the hollows and valleys that had been scoured out by the ice. There are many *eskers*, long winding ridges of sand and gravel deposited by streams which percolated through cracks and passages in the ice and spilled out along the ice front.

Much of southern Finland is sparsely inhabited because the physical environment (lakes, swamp and forest) makes communications difficult and the area inhospitable to settlement and agriculture.

Figure D A glacial erratic of gritstone on a limestone surface. Norbet, Ingleborough, Yorkshire

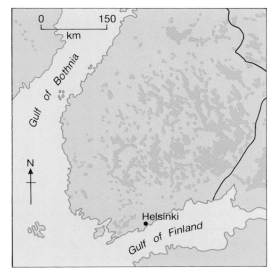

Figure E Southern Finland

QUESTIONS

1 a) In which part of North Wales is Cricieth?
   b) What suggests to you that there might be *two* tills at Cricieth? What could this tell you about how glaciation occurred?

2 a) In which direction are most pebbles in the Cricieth till aligned?
   b) Where do you think the ice which laid down the Cricieth till could have come from?

3 a) Name *three* pieces of evidence you might find in the field of ice deposition that could indicate the direction of ice movement.
   b) Describe how you might use each sort of evidence.
   c) Look back to the previous section on Cwm Idwal. Can you find an *erosional* feature which indicates ice movement direction?

4 a) Explain what is meant by a 'retreating ice sheet'.
   b) What can terminal moraines tell you about ice retreat?

5 Describe how each of the following features may affect patterns of human activity:
   till plains   drumlins   meltwater lakes
   Give an example of a place or area affected in each case.

Figure A Location of the Lule Valley

Figure B Temperature and extent of permafrost

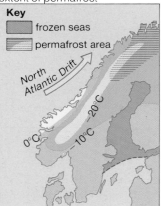

Figure C Vegetation types

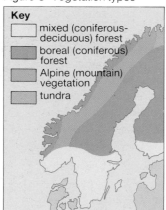

Figure D (*right*) Kiruna, Sweden

The extract below describes the Lule valley, which is in Norbotten, the northernmost county of Sweden. Much of the Lule valley lies within the Arctic Circle. Answer questions 1 and 2 before you read on.

The Lule valley is in one of the coldest places in the world which is inhabited by people. The last glaciation in this area came to an end only 8500 years ago. Because of the high latitude, snowfields and glaciers persist in the mountains all the year round. It would take only a slight fall in average temperatures for ice caps to cover the lowlands again.

The Lule Valley

From October to March the Lule valley experiences the prolonged rigours of sub-Arctic winter, with average daily temperatures well below freezing. Snow will cover the ground for a few months to varying depths depending on shelter and altitude. At this time the sun disappears for several weeks. The soil can be frozen down to 300 m, which limits the amount of water and soil available for plant growth. The winter winds are dry and abrasive to plants.

If we define summer in northern Sweden as the period when average daily temperatures are above 10° C, then it does not begin in the Lule valley until mid-June and lasts until mid-August. Ice will thaw on lakes, rivers will be swollen and fast-flowing, and the surface soil above the permafrost will melt. This summer thaw is deep enough to permit roots to develop and support the trees.

Permafrost

Northern Sweden is *periglacial*. This means that although it is not glaciated, the ground is frozen (*permafrost*) for much of the year. During the short summer the surface layers of the soil thaw enough to permit plant growth in the poorly drained, boggy soil. The growing season however is too short for agriculture. By October the ground is already beginning to freeze again.

This part of Sweden receives only about 400 mm of rain a year because it lies in the rain shadow of the Scandinavian mountains. For much of the year the lower mountain slopes are free of thick snow, but are subject to intense *frost shattering*. Screes of angular boulders build up at the base of slopes.

The natural vegetation of these areas is *boreal forest*, mostly birch and coniferous trees such as pine and spruce. Although the sun is not very strong at these latitudes, the forest grows well because of the long hours of daylight in the summer. Lumbering is the principal economic activity in the Lule valley. Logs are cut in autumn and floated down the river to sawmills. At this time of the year the river is flowing rapidly because of the summer snowmelt.

Kiruna

Kiruna (Figure D) is one of the remotest places in Sweden. It is 1700 km by rail from Stockholm. Kiruna lies about 100 km north of the Lule valley. Its population of 28 000 makes it one of the largest settlements in Arctic Europe. It is also at a higher altitude than any other town in Scandinavia.

The economic importance of Kiruna lies in its iron ore resources. Iron ore mining has been carried on at Kiruna since 1890. Although Kiruna is linked by rail to the Swedish port of Lulea, the main outlet for the ore is through the Norwegian port of Narvik. Unlike Lulea, Narvik is ice-free all the year round. The railway to Narvik is kept

Figure E   A tundra landscape

open all the year, even through the severest winter weather.

The Arctic climate means that working and living in Kiruna is unattractive to many people. In winter there is six weeks of continuous darkness and temperatures may fall as low as −40° C. Snow lingers in the streets until June. High wages have to be offered to people to attract them from the milder and more comfortable south of Sweden. Cheap hydroelectricity means that the population can have high standards of housing and amenities. Even so, few people settle in Kiruna, but usually return southwards after several years

The tundra

Further north still towards the Arctic Ocean the permafrost becomes much thicker. In Siberia the permafrost reaches 1500 m in thickness. The natural vegetation is *tundra*, a covering of low-growing Arctic plants such as mosses, lichens, and low shrubs. These are the only plant forms which can grow in the short Arctic summers and survive in the cold, water-logged soils.

Some 26 per cent of the earth's land surface experiences periglacial conditions. If the world's climate became colder again, these would be the first areas to be glaciated. Other areas lying close to them would in turn become periglacial. In this way global climatic cooling would affect huge areas of the earth's surface and thousands of millions of its peoples.

QUESTIONS

1 What does the extract tell you about:
   a) the length of the summer in Northern Sweden?
   b) daylight in the summer?
   c) daylight in the winter?
   d) the frost-free period?
   e) growth rates of forests and crops?

   Study Figures A–C and your atlases.
   2 Which of the following are *true* and which are *false*?:
   a) The Lule valley lies further south than Iceland
   b) The Lule valley is at the same latitude as the Shetland Islands
   c) All three countries on the sketch map lie partly within the Arctic Circle
   d) Sweden has more of its land within the Arctic Circle than the other two countries.

3 Study the following data:

Average monthly temperature figures for the Lule valley

Month	J	F	M	A	M	J	J	A	S	O	N	D
T°C	−11	−11	−1	−1	4	9	13	10	6	0	−5	−10

   a) Trees are unlikely to grow where the temperature falls below 6° C. For how many weeks of the year is tree growth possible?
   b) For how many weeks of the year is ground in the Lule valley likely to be frozen?

4 **a)** Suggest why Narvik is free of ice all the year round whereas Lulea is not.
   b) What factors contribute to:
      i)   discourage people from working in Kiruna?
      ii) encourage them to work there?

5 What does each of the following tell you about the *climate* of Northern Sweden.:
      permafrost   tundra   frost shattering

6 Study the following data:

Growing season and minimum requirements of certain crops

Crop	Minimum length (days) needed to grow crop	Minimum temperature needed for growth
Barley	85	5.5
Oats	90	7.5
Winter wheat	100	5.0
Spring wheat	105	8.0
Roots	110	8.0

   a) Look back to the data for question 3. Which of the above crops might it be possible to grow in the Lule valley?
   b) Do you think the growth of these crops would be successful? Write a short essay setting out your reasons.

A glaciation model

Figure A is a model drawn to show how glaciation would affect the area shown in the cross-section. Study the model and answer these questions:

1 Name a zone where:
   a) ice is being formed
   b) ice debris is being deposited
   c) meltwater lakes are likely to occur   (3 marks)

2 a) Name a feature which is characteristic of:
   i)   the *upland valley* zone
   ii) the *lowland deposition* zone
   iii) the *permafrost* zone
   b) Describe how each of the features you have named in a) are formed.   (9 marks)

3 a) In which of the following zones might you carry out field work to find the following:
   striations   drumlins   erratics
   b) Explain what you might be able to learn about glaciation from studies of these features.   (9 marks)

4 Explain the *processes* by which:
   a) ice is formed from fallen snow in the *upland valley* zone
   b) debris is deposited to form *terminal moraines*
   c) *icebergs* break away from glaciers   (9 marks)

                                        Total: 30 marks

Glaciation mapwork

Study the 1:50 000 Ordnance Survey map extract (p.126).

1 Find and name the highest point on this map. What is its height?   (1 mark)

2 Find Llynnau Cwmsilin (square 5150). This is an example of a *cwm* (corrie, or cirque).
   a) Which features on the map suggest to you that it might be a cwm?
   b) What other evidence might you look for inside the cwm to indicate that it might have been occupied by ice?
   c) In which direction would the ice have moved out of the cwm? How high is the cwm now above the Nantlle valley?   (6 marks)

3 Study the lowland area to the west of the National Park boundary:
   a) Would you describe it as flat, gently sloping, or uneven?
   b) Suggest a reason for the character of the surface. What features of past glaciation might you expect to find?
   c) Suggest which zone on the model above could be applicable to this area.   (6 marks)

4 How do you think the former glaciation of this area might be affecting the ways man is using it?   (7 marks)

                                        Total: 20 marks

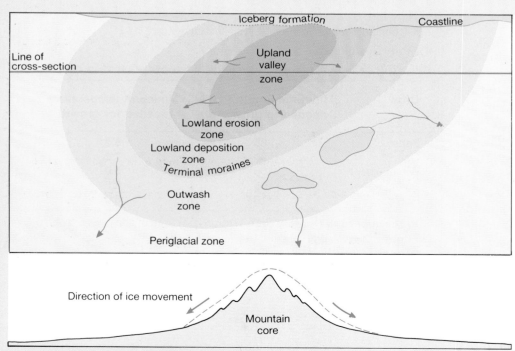

Some features of glacial zones

Upland valley zone
Cwms (corries, cirques), arêtes, U-shaped valleys, hanging valleys

Lowland valley zone
Ice-scoured rock surfaces, ice sheets formed by joined-up glaciers

Lowland deposition zone
Till plains, drumlins, eskers, (formed by sub-glacial streams)

Outwash zone
Meltwater lakes, meltwater sands and gravels

Periglacial zone
Permafrost

Figure A A model of the effects of glaciation on a mountain area

Ice and cold in Northern Europe

Figure B shows some of the Northern Hemisphere:

1 At which of the places 1–5 might you expect to find the following:
   a) an ice cap covering most of the land mass?
   b) frozen ground for much of the year?
   c) seas free of ice in winter?
   d) icebergs that are a hazard to shipping?
   e) boreal forest?
   f) boreal forest with many lakes?   (6 marks)

2 Locations **X**, **Y**, and **Z** on the map are under consideration by an international winter sports company for the development of a new ski and winter sports centre. It expects the new centre to be used mainly by visitors from North America, Britain, and Western Europe.
   a) Using atlases and the information in these units, make a list of the factors the company should be taking into account in making its decision.
   b) Can you help the company to come to a decision about which place would be the best location?   (4 marks)

          Total: 20 marks

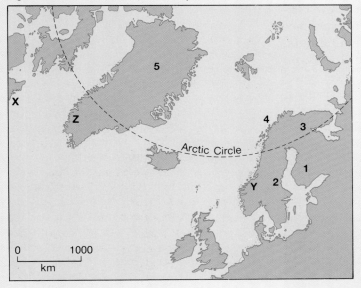

Figure B Part of the Northern Hemisphere

Details for pupil profile sheets Unit 6

Knowledge and understanding

1 Glaciation and climate – climatic change, interglacial periods
2 Processes of ice mass formation – ice-caps, glaciers, icebergs
3 Upland erosional features – corries (cwms), U-shaped valleys, etc.
4 Lowland depositional features – till plains, terminal moraines, meltwater features, etc.
5 Periglacial features – permafrost, tundra and forest vegetation

Skills

1 Interpretation of ice and iceberg patterns from satellite imagery
2 Interpretation of patterns of ice movement from field evidence – observations, sketching, till fabric analysis
3 Interpretation of patterns of ice movement from OS maps
4 Glacial model testing

Values

1 Awareness of value of glaciers for leisure activities, educational purposes
2 Awareness of ice masses as a hazard to human activity
3 Awareness of limitations of cold conditions to human activity – mining, farming

Figure A Offshore rocks and a promontory mark the position of the old coastline near Lulworth Cove

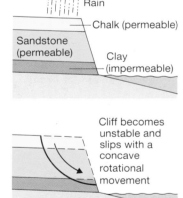

Figure B How cliffs collapse by rotational slip

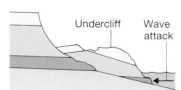

Figure C Newborough Warren on Ynys Mon (Anglesey)

Figure A shows a line of rocks off the south coast of England. These rocks mark the most resistant parts of an old coastline. They were left behind after the rest of the coast was worn away by *wave action*.

Another cause of retreat of a coastline is *rotational slip* (Figure B). The slippage is brought about not by wave attack but by the saturation of the upper part of the cliff by rainwater. Weathering and gullying of the cliff face also make it less stable.

Some coastlines are not retreating. Where the waves and tides deposit more sediment onshore than they wash away, the coast gradually builds outwards. Much of it will be made up of sand-dunes, or of mud-flats and marshes which are only submerged at very high tides (Figure C).

Changing sea levels

A rise in sea level of only a few centimetres would cause the *submergence* of large tracts of beaches or mud-flats, and lead to stronger wave attack on cliffs. A similar fall in sea level could result in the *emergence* of the coast. If waves were unable to reach the base of cliffs, cliff erosion would cease.

It is thought that about 10 000 years ago, Britain was joined to the European continent (Figure D). Since then many of our coasts have retreated. The retreat has been caused by a rise in sea level following the melting of the ice caps after the last Ice Age.

In Devon this rise in sea-level has produced many *rias*, or drowned river valleys (Figure E). Rias form wide estuaries with many inlets, and extend for several kilometres inland.

In Norway long arms of the sea called *fiords* penetrate inland for several kilometres (Figure F). These are drowned glaciated valleys. The valleys were formed during the Ice Ages by glaciers from the Norwegian mountains. As the ice-caps melted, sea level rose and the coastal valleys were flooded. Around the edges of fiords there is very little space for settlement or cultivation.

Figure D The coastline of Britain 10 000 years ago

Figure E (*top*) The Salcombe estuary, a ria
Figure F (*above*) Geiranger Fiord, Norway

Coastlines in balance

On any coast at any one time many processes are at work. Their relative strengths will decide whether the coast retreats, advances, or stays where it is. A stable coast, neither advancing or retreating, represents a state of balance or *equilibrium* between all the processes.

Sometimes people can upset this equilibrium. At Hallsands in Devon in about 1900, 650 000 tonnes of shingle were dredged off the shore to use to build Devonport dockyard. The dredging lowered the beach, allowing storm waves to reach much further inshore. The storm waves destroyed the beach from which the fishermen had used to launch their boats. In 1917 a great storm destroyed most of the village behind the beach. People had not realized the importance of the shingle in the balance of coastal forces.

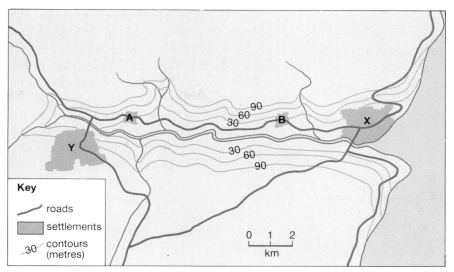

Figure G Sketch map for question 3

QUESTIONS

1 a) Describe *two* ways in which a coastline can be worn away
  b) Describe *two* opposite ways in which changes in sea level affect coasts.

2 Complete the following diagram by inserting the words *outbuilding*, *submergence*, and *erosion/weathering* in the correct boxes:

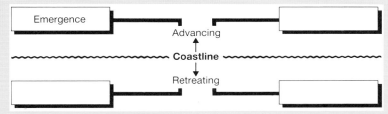

Figure H Coastal movement diagram

3 a) Make a copy of the sketch map (Figure G) showing a river valley and coast.
  b) Assume that a rise in sea level of 60 metres occurs. Shade in the area that will be drowned by the sea.
  c) Measure the length and width of the ria you have formed
  d) Describe the effects of the rise in sea level on the people living in the area.
  e) From the map of Britain's coastline, name an area which might have experienced changes like this.

4 Describe *three* ways by which you can distinguish a ria from a fiord.

5 Write a letter, as from a resident of Hallsands to a relative elsewhere, explaining the changes that occurred to local people at the beginning of the century.

6 What evidence would you put forward to support the following:
  a) Changes in sea level cause major, long-term changes in the coastline
  b) Wave action causes only minor, short-term changes.

7.2 Waves and rocks

Figure A Wave features

Measurable properties of waves

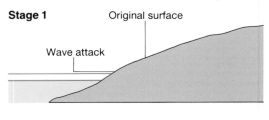

Key

h = wave height (metres)
L = wave length (metres)
T = wave period (seconds)

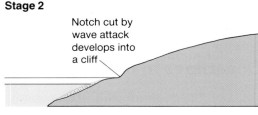

Strong wind   Gentle wind

Plunging breaker   Spilling breaker

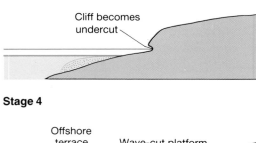

Gentle beach   Steep beach   Cliff

Figure B Handfast Point

Wave attack from both sides has eroded and divided headland

Arches and caves

Stack

Sea spray weathers cliff face

Base of rock under continual wave attack

Wave-cut platform

Waves gain their energy from the strength of the wind. Waves produced by strong winds will be deep compared with their length, and will break on the shore every few seconds. Under calm conditions however the waves will be shallow and there will be long intervals between them. Figure A shows the relationship between *wave height*, *length*, and *period*. Deep, strong waves are likely to be produced where the wind blows over many kilometres of open ocean. The distance over which the wave has been formed is called the *fetch*.

How waves attack cliffs

In the picture of Handfast Point (Figure B) the sea is calm. In stormy weather *plunging* breakers (Figure A) batter the cliff. As they hit the rocks they trap and compress air in cracks and crevices, exerting *hydraulic pressure*. When the pressure is released the air expands and explodes outwards. This breaks off loose pieces of rock and enlarges the cracks. The waves also throw rock fragments and pebbles against the cliff face, eroding it by *abrasion*. Salt crystals formed from the spray lodge in cracks and break down the minerals in the rocks by *chemical weathering*.

Most erosion and weathering takes place at the base of the cliff, which is constantly scoured by the sea even in calm conditions. Figure C shows some wave-cut features and how they are formed. By the time stage 4 is reached the cliff will be relatively stable. Look for vegetation growing on cliff faces; this usually indicates that wave attack has ceased.

Hard and soft rocks

Figure D shows a section of coastline. Notice how different bands of rock reach the coast at right angles. The harder, more resistant rocks have been left as *headlands* while the softer rocks have been worn back to form *bays*.

Stage 1

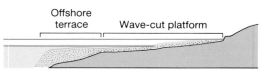

Original surface

Wave attack

Stage 2

Notch cut by wave attack develops into a cliff

Stage 3

Cliff becomes undercut

Stage 4

Offshore terrace   Wave-cut platform

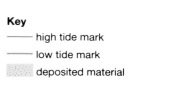

Key

—— high tide mark
—— low tide mark
∙∙∙∙∙ deposited material

Figure C How a cliff retreats to produce a wave-cut platform

The headlands are under severe wave attack. As the waves approach the headlands they meet the shallow sea floor offshore. The contour lines beneath the sea are parallel with the headlands. They cause the waves to bend round so that they meet the shore head on. This is called *wave refraction*. You can see how wave refraction causes wave energy to become concentrated on the headlands. The energy of the waves in the bay is spread out over a long length of coastline.

Caves, arches, and stacks

The sea will easily find points of weakness in coastal rocks. Faults, joints or cracks can often be scoured by the sea and enlarged to form *caves*. On headlands caves may be driven into the rocks from both sides and eventually meet to form an *arch*. In time the arch will become unstable from wave attack and will collapse to leave an isolated rock in the sea, called a *stack*. Find these features in Figure A. The cliffs in this picture are made of chalk, which is a well-jointed rock and therefore is easily eroded.

QUESTIONS

1 Name *three* properties of a wave that can be measured.
2 Describe *three* ways in which the sea can attack the face of a cliff.
3 Explain why:
   a) the profile of a cliff may gradually change
   b) there is often a concentration of wave attack on headlands
   c) arches and stacks may develop along coastlines of well-jointed rocks.
4 The following table was made up from data on wave type brought back by pupils from a fieldwork location. Copy and complete it.
   Wave type recording table

Wave height (m)	Wave period (secs)	Beach slope (deg)	Breaker type
0.8	5	10	plunging
0.3	12	3	
0.8	12	cliff	

5 Make a sketch of Figure B, such as you might draw in the field. On your sketch carefully label
   a) the coastal features   **b)** the processes causing them
6 Look at pages 68–79 again. Explain what might happen to the stable cliff in Figure C if the level of the sea gradually rose several feet over a period of many hundreds of years.

Fieldwork
7 Fieldwork along the coast may be hazardous, especially in bad weather. *Never* work out of the sight of your supervising teacher and keep well out of the range of deep water and heavy seas.
   a) Project 1
   Make a sketch of suitable views of coastal cliffs and other features mentioned on these pages. Label your sketch. Compare sketches of different locations and write about how the processes acting upon the cliffs vary.
   b) Project 2
   i) Obtain some long poles and mark them off into easily readable sections of a metre and parts of a metre.
   ii) Working from a safe concrete or stone breakwater, use the poles to measure the height of incoming waves. Record the data in a table.
   iii) At the same time measure the period between each breaking wave, and also record it.
   iv) Use the poles to estimate beach angle (e.g. 1 in 30).
   v) Carry out i) and ii) several times and average out the results.
   vi) From your results write about how breaker type varies according to beach angle and wave strength.

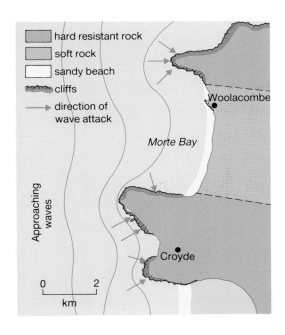

Figure D A coastline in North Devon. Wave energy is concentrated on the headlands.

7.3
Drifting beaches

The fence-like structures extending out into the sea at Sherringham (Figure A) are called *groynes*. Groynes are often found on holiday resort beaches. They have been placed there to stop the *longshore drift* of sand and shingle. It is important for holiday resorts to conserve their sand in order to keep the beaches attractive.

Beach material accumulates on the shore because of *wave deposition*. Gentle waves with spilling breakers will tend to move sand and pebbles on to the shore, piling it up into beaches. But waves also contribute to the *transportation* of beach material. Look at Figure B which shows how waves move material along the shore. In practice, longshore drift patterns can be much more complicated. Heavy pebbles may only be moved very occasionally. As the prevailing wind changes in direction a single pebble may be shifted first one way and then the other.

Spits

Sometimes longshore drift transports beach material across the mouth of a bay or the estuary of a river. Here a long line of sand or shingle called a *spit* will grow. Marshes, lagoons, or mudflats may develop behind the spit. The spit may not be able to completely block off the river because of the scour created by the river outflow. However if the longshore drift is very strong and the river is weak, the mouth of the river might be diverted for several miles along the shore.

Figure C is a map of the coast of East Anglia near Great Yarmouth. The cliffs to the north of Great Yarmouth along the coast are made of boulder clay and easily crumble. Longshore drift has

Figure A Groynes along the coast at Sheringham, Norfolk

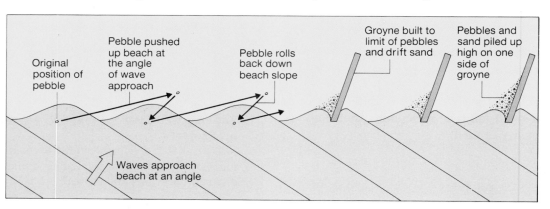

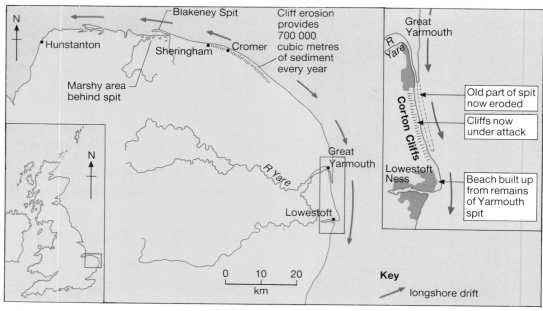

Figure B (*top right*) How longshore drift occurs

Figure C (*right*) Cliff erosion and spits in Norfolk. The inset shows the Yarmouth spit

moved much of this material southwards and built up the spit across the mouth of the River Yare at Great Yarmouth.

Centuries ago the Yarmouth spit was several miles longer than it is now. Yarmouth fishermen breached the spit in order to get their boats out to sea more easily. Figure C shows what effects this had.

Beaches and beach profiles

The cross-profile of a beach varies according to the dominant types of breakers and the size of the beach material. Sandy beaches subjected to gentle spilling breakers have a very gentle gradient, perhaps not more than 1 in 30. Shingle beaches attacked by plunging breakers can be much steeper, anything up to 1 in 4.

The cross-profile (Figure D) is a model for a very varied beach, with both sand and shingle, subjected to different sorts of breakers. Any actual beach you study might vary in some detail from this 'model' one. The next section shows you some of the ways in which you can learn more about how a beach has been formed by studying its material.

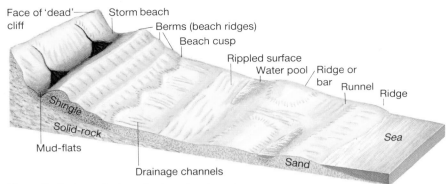

Figure D Features that can be found on beaches

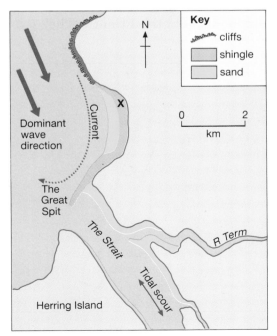

Figure E Sketch map for question 4

QUESTIONS

1 Study the cross-profile below of a typical beach. Write the following in the correct boxes:

storm ridge   foreshore   beach ridges   dunes

2 a) What is a groyne?
   b) What purpose do groynes serve?
   c) Why is there more sand on one side of a groyne than on the other?

3 From the map of East Anglia (Figure C) name a place:
   a) where waves have only recently been eroding cliffs
   b) where cliffs provide large quantities of beach sediment
   c) where holidaymakers will benefit from sand deposition
   d) which was once an outlet for a river.

4 Study Figure E, a map of a coastline.
   a) Suggest where the material for spit development is likely to have come from.
   b) Explain why the spit has developed in a easterly direction.
   c) Why is the spit unlikely to grow long enough to join the island to the mainland?
   d) How might the direction of spit growth change in the future?
   e) Suppose the shingle at **X** was quarried for building material. What impact might this have on the spit?

Fieldwork

5 You will probably be able to carry out this project only if you live close to the coast and some shingle beaches.
   a) Paint a sample of about a hundred pebbles from the beach and leave them to dry.
   b) Select a clear stretch of foreshore away from groynes. Leave the pebbles on the beach, making a careful note of their exact location. Record wind direction.
   c) Check changes in wind direction over the next few days.
   d) After five days try to find your pebbles. How many can you find? Note their locations carefully. How far have they drifted? In what direction? Have the smaller ones drifted further? How does the pattern of drift reflect wave movements?

The map and photograph show Chesil Beach in Dorset. This beach is a long spit of shingle joining the Isle of Portland to the mainland. A spit which joins an island to the mainland is called a *tombolo*.

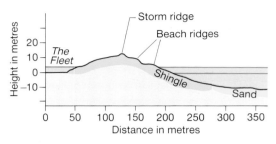

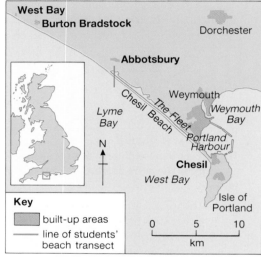

Figure A (*Top right*) Cross-profile and (*right*) location of Chesil Beach

Figure B Two views of Chesil Beach from the Isle of Portland showing how the beach changes

A party of students carried out field work at three locations along the beach – Chesil (Portland), Abbotsbury and Burton Bradstock (see Figure A). At each location they first looked at their Ordnance Survey maps and wrote down how far they were from the Portland end of the beach. They then carried out these tasks:

● Using surveying poles (Figure C) they measured the height of the highest part of the beach above the high tide level.

● Working in groups they used a 'pebbleometer' (Figure D) to calculate the average size of a sample of pebbles.

● Finally they looked at the beach profile and counted the number of beach ridges between the tide level and the storm ridge which formed the summit.

Figure D summarises the students' results. Study these and answer questions **1–3** before you go on reading.

Explaining the results

The map (Figure E) showing wind directions helps to explain why pebble size and beach height vary along the beach. For most of the time Chesil Beach is in the path of strong south-westerly winds coming in from the Atlantic. They pro-

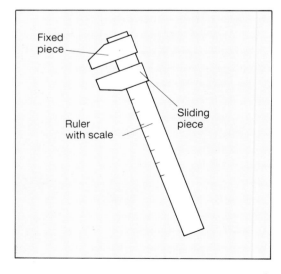

Figure C A pebbleometer

duce a southward longshore drift of material, moving both large and small pebbles. This builds up the beach at the Portland end.

Some of the time, however, milder winds blow onshore from a southerly direction. They cause a northward longshore drift of smaller pebbles.

The overall result is that gradually a grading of pebble size has been taking place along the beach, with the biggest pebbles becoming more concentrated at the Portland end. Here the beach has been built up very high by the waves. Local fishermen say they can tell where they are on the beach just by looking at the size of the pebbles.

Geographers now think that Chesil Beach has not been formed by longshore drift, only modified by it. They think that most of its material was washed inshore by a rise in sea level. This happened at the end of the last Ice Age. Longshore drift has gradually been shifting material backwards and forwards along the beach, grading it by pebble size in the way described above.

Figure D Results of a students' survey of Chesil Beach

Measurement	Chesil (Portland)	Abbotsbury	Burton Bradstock
Distance from end of beach (km)	0.0	14.0	20.0
Height of highest part of beach above high tide level (m)	13.0	7.0	5.0
Average size of pebbles (cm)	7.0	3.0	2.5
Number of beach ridges	3.0	2.0	9.0

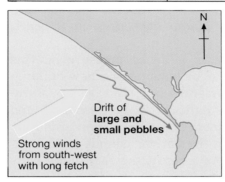
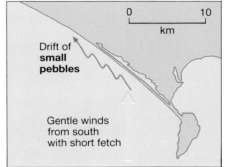

Figure E The effect of wind direction on pebble movement

QUESTIONS

1 What is the height of the beach at:
   a) Chesil? **b)** Burton Bradstock?

2 Describe how the average size of pebbles varies from one end of the beach to the other.

3 Which end of the beach is most affected by storm waves? Why?

4 Figure F shows Sea Areas used in fishing forecasts.
   a) On a copy of this map continue to draw parallel lines showing winds coming from the south-west.
   b) Which Sea Areas around Britain are most at risk from Atlantic winds?
   c) Shade in stretches of coastline which are in the path of winds with an Atlantic fetch.
   d) With the help of an atlas name *three* holiday resorts likely to experience deep waves for much of the year.

5 Design a warning poster to be displayed at several points on Chesil Beach, explaining to visitors why swimming there can be dangerous.

Fieldwork

6 'Pebbles on the lower part of a beach should be more rounded than those on the upper beach'.
   a) Write a paragraph explaining why you think this hypothesis might be true.
   b) Using a pebbleometer collect and measure a sample of pebbles from the upper and lower parts of a beach.
   c) Test the statement above using the data you have collected. Does it seem to be true in the case of your beach?

Figure F Sea Areas around the British Isles

7.5
Managing coasts

Barrier islands

The coast of North Carolina, USA, is very flat. Long, broad sand banks form *barrier islands* several miles offshore (Figure A). These islands have wide beaches and dune belts, and are separated from each other by tidal channels. Behind the dunes and beaches are shallow sounds and marshes (Figures B and C) rich in wildlife. These inlets and marshes are used for hunting, fishing, and leisure. Along the islands are hotels, piers, harbours, and beach chalets.

There is a lot of pressure on this coastline for housing and new building developments. But, this coast is frequently battered by heavy storms and hurricanes. These have been gradually pushing the barrier islands further inshore. As a result the sand dune belts have moved landwards. For a long time people have tried to find ways of stopping the dune belts from moving inland. Between 1936 and 1940, 1 000 km of 'sand fences' were built along the outer banks. These fences were intended to give the sand something to build itself up against. Once established these dunes were then 'fixed' by planting trees and grasses. In this way some dunes were stabilized (Figure B).

But there were some unexpected side-effects. The natural barrier islands had absorbed and dispersed the wave energy from violent storms. The higher, narrower beaches produced by the sand fences made the storm waves break more violently, causing increased coastal erosion. They also produced a lot more flooding in Pamlico Sound behind the dune belt.

More coastal protection

In 1964 the coastal protection authority decided that it must do a lot more to protect the coast from further retreat, otherwise the livelihoods of businesses and the homes of residents would be at risk. New sea walls, sand fences, jetties, groynes, rubble barriers, and other sea defences were built. Attempts were also made to stop tidal inlets from changing in position so that bridges would not be threatened.

Despite these measures the coast still continued to retreat. A few years ago the authority changed its mind about how to deal with the problem. After studying the coastline more carefully it was decided to let the natural processes take their course. Instead, new building developments were discouraged, and fewer sand fences were built.

The change in policy about the barrier islands shows that people have learned something about coastal management. The earlier policy was not very successful because the authorities hadn't properly understood how the coastal processes operated. They had failed to realise that although the coast

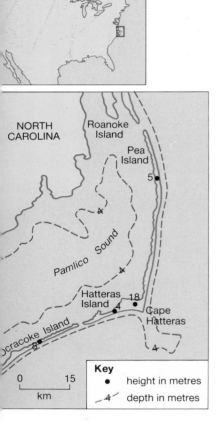

Figure A Location of the Barrier Islands off the coast of North Carolina, USA

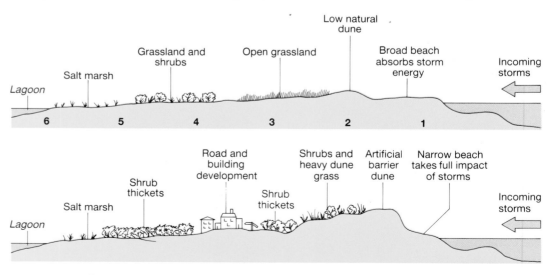

Figure B Sections across an Island: a) before and b) after building developments and barrier dunes

was retreating it acted as a good natural defence system against incoming storms. The natural broad beaches and dune belts were much better at breaking up the energy of the storms than the man-made sand fences, walls and barriers.

Figure D describes stages in the interaction between coastlines and people. Which stage has the coastline of North Carolina reached? Do you think all coastlines have reached this stage? Think about a stretch of coastline you know. What stage does it appear to have reached?

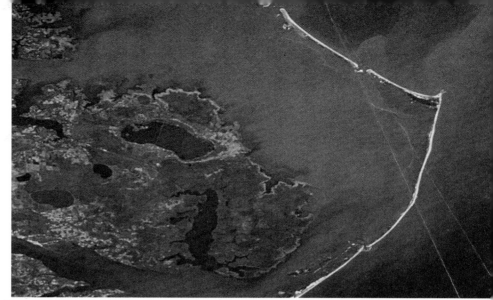

Figure C The Barrier Islands from the air with Pamlico Sound and marshland behind them

Figure D Coasts and people

Stage 1	Little or no human interference
Coastline shaped entirely by natural processes.
Human activity limited to traditional livelihoods, for example, fishing, which makes little change to the coast

Stage 2   Interference from elsewhere
Human activity further along the coast or off-shore begins to modify the coastline. For example:
- beach protection measures down shore cut off the supply of shingle by longshore drift; this exposes cliffs to stronger wave attack
- dredging deeper channels for ships downshore cuts off the supply of shingle
- soil erosion inland results in more silt in rivers and increases supply of beach material; waves now break further out

Stage 3   Exploitation
Intensive use of the coast for building developments, industry, leisure, holiday resorts
Coastal system seriously disturbed by man, for example, groynes disrupt pattern of longshore drift, building sea walls causes lowering of beach

Stage 4   Management
People more aware of impact of human activity on coast
Developments and protection measures designed not to disturb coastal system

QUESTIONS

1 What is:
  a) the distance between Hatteras Island and the mainland?
  b) the height of Ocracoke Island?
  c) the depth of Pamlico Sound off Pea Island?

2 How have the following influenced the growth and development of the barrier islands:
  a) gentle beaches?
  b) hurricanes?
  c) sand fences?
  d) building developments?

3 a) Using the numbers on the cross-section, complete the table below:

Changes that have taken place on the barrier islands

Number on cross-section	Before human interference	After human interference
1 2 3 4 5 6		

  b) Using the table, describe the changes in the barrier islands that people have brought about.

4 Study Figure D.
  a) What stage has been reached by:
    i)   the Barrier Islands?
    ii)   a coastline you have studied for fieldwork?
  b) What information suggests to you that coasts can be altered by:
    i)   coastal changes elsewhere?
    ii)   changes in river basins elsewhere?

Unit 7 ASSESSMENT

What you know

1 Name *two* sorts of valleys which can be formed by submergence of the coast. Explain how each is formed. (4 marks)

2 Describe how each of the following can cause coastal erosion:
   hydraulic pressure   abrasion
   chemical weathering
   (6 marks)

3 What are groynes? What are they for? Describe what they look like. (2 marks)

4 Draw and label a picture of a device you could use to measure the size of pebbles. (3 marks)

5 Name an area of the world where artificial dunes have been developed to try to prevent coastal retreat. (2 marks)

6 Explain the role of the following in rotational slip along sea cliffs:
   a) rainwater
   b) type of rock
   c) waves   (6 marks)

7 Draw cross-profiles through a cliff to show:
   a) features of a cliff under regular attack by the sea,
   b) features of a cliff which the sea is no longer attacking   (6 marks)

8 a) What is meant by wave height?
   b) How does it affect the ways in which waves break on reaching the shore? (4 marks)

9 Describe a case you have studied in which human activity has influenced spit development. (4 marks)

10 Explain why the strength of waves is dependent on their fetch. Give examples. (4 marks)

11 Explain what is meant by equilibrium along the coastline. Find *three* examples of where this equilibrium has been disturbed by people. For each case describe a problem for man which resulted. (6 marks)

12 On a copy map of southern England locate and name the case studies used for this area in the 'Along the Coast' units. For each location add labels to show:
   a) the dominant coastal processes taking place
   b) any human problems which may be occurring.
   (8 marks)
   Total: 55 marks

Figure A Part of the British coastline

What you understand

Study the sketch map of a section of coastline.

1 Name the *four* features of the coastline labelled A–D by choosing from the following list:
   headland   stack   tombolo   cave
   spit   bay   arch   wave-cut platform (4 marks)

2 From the map evidence, identify the direction of longshore drift between
   a) A and C
   b) C and E   (2 marks)

3 What map evidence suggests that this might be a submerged coastline? (3 marks)

4 List the different ways in which people appear to be making use of this coastline. (6 marks)

5 Suggest how the following are likely to be influencing the development of the coastline at C:
   wave action   rock structure   human activity
   (6 marks)

6 You are on a walking holiday along this stretch of coastline. Write a letter to a friend describing how the scenery changes along the coast path between A and F. (6 marks)

7 There is a proposal by a building firm to quarry shingle from the beach at D. Explain how this would affect:
   a) the natural development of the coastline
   b) other human activities in the area   (4 marks)

8 Explain a technique you could use to learn more about
   a) wave patterns at B   b) beach sediments at E.
   (4 marks)
   Total: 35 marks

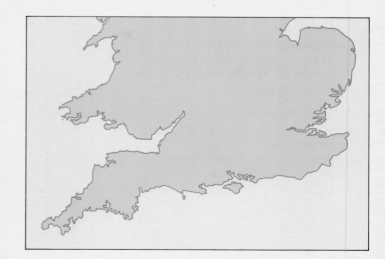

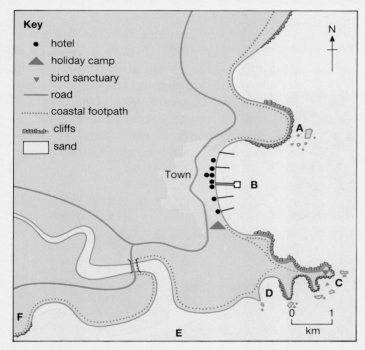

Key

- • hotel
- ▲ holiday camp
- ▼ bird sanctuary
- —— road
- ········ coastal footpath
- cliffs
- ☐ sand

N

Town

A

B

C

D

E

F

0   1

km

Figure B Sketch map of a section of coastline

Details for pupil profile sheets Unit 7

Knowledge and understanding

1 Wave motion and wave action
2 Non-marine processes, e.g. rotational slip
3 Coastal submergence, emergence, erosion, outbuilding
4 Coastal equilibrium
5 Cliff retreat under wave attack; headlands, bays, caves, arches, stacks
6 Transportation and deposition: beaches, groynes
7 Transportation and deposition: longshore drift, spits
8 Beach sediments: pebble size and roundness
9 Coastal protection measures: coastal management

Skills

1 Testing ideas on coastal change from evidence supplied
2 Writing a descriptive letter
3 Testing model of beach profile
4 Measurements of distance from map
5 Use of aerial photograph/satellite image
6 Fieldwork: sketching outdoors
7 Fieldwork: measuring wave height and period
8 Fieldwork: measuring rate of longshore drift
9 Fieldwork: measuring beach height
10 Fieldwork: measuring pebble size and roundness
11 Interpretation of data collected from field studies

Values

1 Awareness of the complexity of natural processes operating along the coastline
2 Awareness of how human activity can disturb natural coastline processes
3 Awareness of the coast as a resource to be carefully managed

Unit 8: What's in the air

'You can't depend on the weather forecast. It's always wrong.'

Anyone who remembers the hurricane of October 1987 (Figure A) will probably agree with this remark. But weather forecasting has become more accurate in recent years. One reason is that forecasters can now depend on information from space. Satellite photographs like the one in Figure B, show

Figure A Hurricane damage, October 1987

Figure B a satellite weather photograph. The white patches are areas of cloud

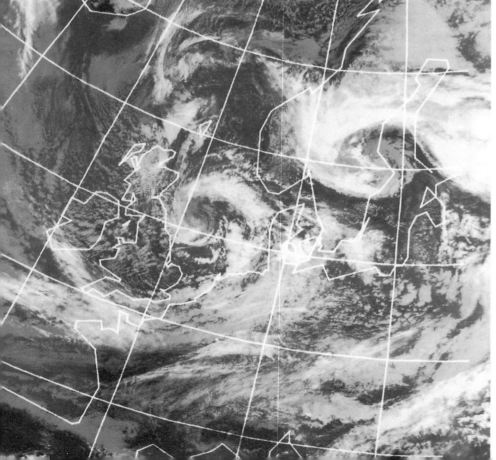

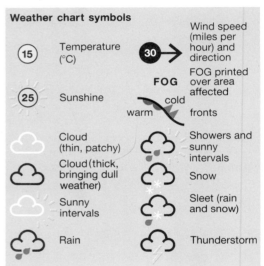

Weather chart symbols

(15)	Temperature (°C)	(30)→	Wind speed (miles per hour) and direction
(25)	Sunshine	**FOG**	FOG printed over area affected
		cold / warm fronts	fronts
	Cloud (thin, patchy)		Showers and sunny intervals
	Cloud (thick, bringing dull weather)		Snow
	Sunny intervals		Sleet (rain and snow)
	Rain		Thunderstorm

Synoptic chart symbols

WIND Symbol	Wind speed (knots)	CLOUD Symbol	Cloud amount (oktas)	Symbol	Cloud amount (oktas)
◎	Calm	○	0	◖	6
	1–2	◑	1 or less	◗	7 or more
	2–7	◕	2	●	8
*	8–12	◔	3	⊗	Sky obscured usually by fog
	13–17	◐	4	⊗	Missing or doubtful data
◄	48–52	◒	5		

*For each additional half-feather add 5 knots

Weather

Symbol	Weather	Symbol	Weather	Symbol	Weather
═	Mist	⚹	Rain and snow	⇧	Hail shower
≡	Fog	✳	Snow	⚡	Thunderstorm
�	Drizzle	▽	Rain shower	─	Warm front
	Rain and drizzle	▽	Rain and snow shower	▲	Cold front
○	Rain	✳▽	Snow shower		Occluded front

Pressure is shown by isobars. These are lines joining places of equal pressure. Pressure is measured in millibars.

Figure C Symbols used on weather maps

Figure D Weather forecasts for a bank holiday weekend in May

accurately the position of masses of clouds and enable forecasters to pick out critical weather features like *fronts* and *pressure systems*. These features directly control conditions such as temperature and rainfall. By studying sequences of satellite pictures taken at regular intervals, forecasters can build up a picture of how the weather pattern is developing. They produce weather maps called *synoptic charts*. Special symbols are used to show weather conditions (Figure C).

A television weather report

The series of pictures in Figure D is taken from a television daily weather report. The report went out on a Friday evening in May. Because it was a long weekend the presenter talked about the weather in European holiday areas as well as in Britain. Study the weather maps and the presenter's comments on them.

QUESTIONS

The following questions relate to the weekend described in Figure D. You may need to use your atlases to help you.

1 Describe how the weather will be over the weekend:
   a) in Scotland and Ireland
   b) in Norway and Sweden
   c) in Turkey and the eastern Mediterranean.

2 Name an area of Britain where:
   a) fog can be expected on Friday evening
   b) thunder might occur on Friday evening
   c) it could be misty on Saturday afternoon
   d) the temperature on Saturday afternoon could rise to 17° C
   e) wind speed on Saturday afternoon will be as low as 10 miles per hour.

3 On an outline map of the British Isles:
   a) draw a line dividing places with temperatures of 11° C and under on Saturday afternoon from those with higher temperatures
   b) draw a line dividing places with temperatures of 15° C and higher on Saturday afternoon from those with lower temperatures
   c) shade in your three temperature zones with different colours
   d) locate and name the following holiday resorts on your map:
   Blackpool   Torquay   Oban
   Margate   Bridlington
   e) give your map a key and title
   f) for *one* of the resorts named in **d)** write a paragraph describing in detail how the weather will change through the weekend.
   Compare it with the weather expected in your home area. Would it be worth going away for the weekend?

8.2 Measuring the weather

The device shown in Figure A can be bought from a garden shop or hobbies shop. It provides an inexpensive way of measuring basic weather characteristics (Figure B).

Look carefully at the weather meter and at the properties it is able to measure. It can provide simple measurements of *temperature*, *wind speed*, *wind direction*, and *total rainfall* over a period of time. It also provides a chart for working out the *wind chill* effect. This is the cooling effect of wind on temperature. It is more fully explained on page 92.

Your school may have more precise instruments for measuring the weather. Some of them are shown on the opposite page. Others may be too expensive for your school to have, but are used regularly in weather stations around the country.

The thermometers are most accurate when they are kept inside a type of box called a *Stevenson screen* (Figure C). This reduces the effect of direct sunlight on the temperature readings and avoids the wind-chill effect. Some schools have Stevenson screens which they have bought in kit form and assembled in the craft workshop.

Figure A A weather meter that can be used at home

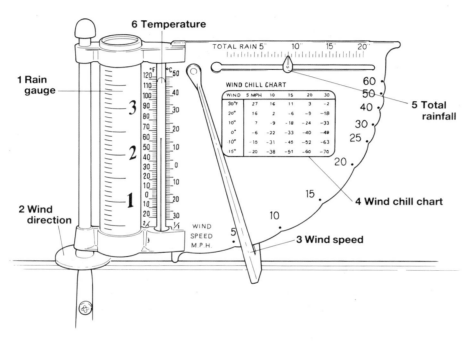

Figure B Measurable properties of weather

Property	Units of measurement	Device or instrument
Temperature	°C – degrees Centigrade (or °F – degrees Fahrenheit on some instruments)	Maximum and minimum thermometer
Humidity	% – per cent	Hygrometer
Rainfall	mm – millimetres (or inches)	Rain gauge
Sunshine	hours per day	Sunshine recorder
Wind speed	km/h – kilometres per hour	Anemometer
Wind direction	points of compass	Wind vane
Pressure	mb – millibars	Aneroid barometer
Cloud cover	oktas (eighths of sky)	Observation

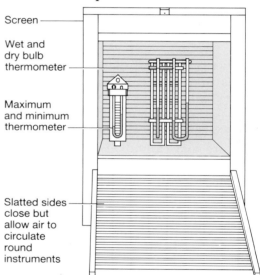

Figure C A Stevenson screen

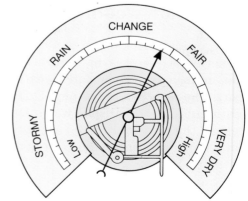

Number of discs in a partial vacuum move with changes of air pressure. This causes the pointer to move over a scale.

Figure D A barometer

Rain gauge

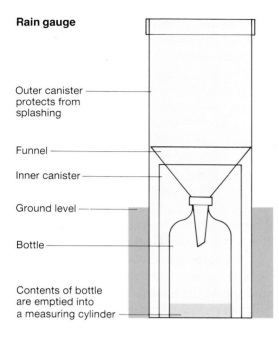

Outer canister protects from splashing

Funnel

Inner canister

Ground level

Bottle

Contents of bottle are emptied into a measuring cylinder

Anemometer

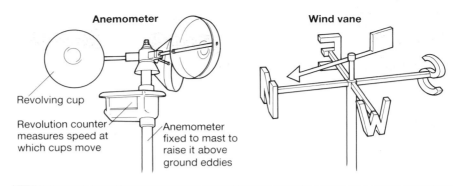

Revolving cup

Revolution counter measures speed at which cups move

Anemometer fixed to mast to raise it above ground eddies

Wind vane

Maximum and minimum thermometer

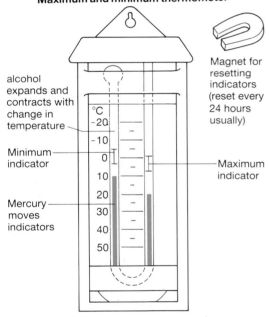

alcohol expands and contracts with change in temperature

Minimum indicator

Mercury moves indicators

Magnet for resetting indicators (reset every 24 hours usually)

Maximum indicator

Whirling hygrometer

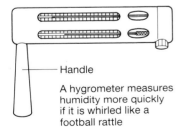

Handle

A hygrometer measures humidity more quickly if it is whirled like a football rattle

Figure E Other instruments for measuring weather

QUESTIONS

1 Name *one* weather instrument or device that is used to measure:
   a) rainfall   b) sunshine   c) wind speed

2 Which properties of the weather could you:
   a) measure using the 'weather meter' at home?
   b) measure only with more specialist instruments?
   c) measure from simple observation?
   d) measure inside a Stevenson screen?
   e) measure using the equipment available at your school?

3 Which weather properties are likely to be of particular interest to:
   a) holidaymakers at a seaside resort?
   b) a farmer hoping his crops will ripen?
   c) an air traffic controller at an airport?
   Give a reason in each case.

Fieldwork

4 You may be able to carry out this project at home or at school depending on the instruments you have available. It will be spread over several weeks. It will be most valuable in late autumn (November to December) or early spring (February to May)
   a) Draw up a recording chart with the following headings:
   ● Date
   ● Minimum temperature recorded
   ● Maximum temperature recorded
   ● Mean daily temperature (average of min. and max.)
   ● Occurrence of early morning frost (yes or no)
   ● Pressure
   Make the chart long enough for several weeks of measurement.
   b) Using a maximum/minimum thermometer and an aneroid barometer, take readings and fill in your chart regularly over the time period you choose.
   c) Ask your teacher about the best way to draw a graph which shows how the following changed during the period of your project:
   minimum daily temperature   mean daily temperature
   frost occurrence   pressure
   d) Describe how the weather patterns changed over your time period.
   e) Write about how the following might help to explain your results:
   i) In winter, high pressure brings dry but cold conditions
   ii) Early morning frost is more likely to occur with high pressure rather than low pressure. High pressure brings clear night skies and rapid loss of heat upwards.

All the energy required for movement of the air in the atmosphere comes from the sun. We can think of the atmosphere as a massive engine powered by inputs of the sun's heat.

Rising and sinking air

If you look above the surface of the road on a hot day, you may notice a heat haze. This is caused by the rising hot air. The air rises because the heat of the sun makes it expand. As it expands it becomes light and buoyant compared with air around it which may not have been heated as much. The less-dense air rises. This process is called *convection*.

Moisture from evaporation from ponds, streams, the soil, and other surfaces may make the air feel 'sticky' and make physical exercise or work tiring.

As the air rises it begins to cool, and eventually the moisture will *condense* to form clouds. The temperature at which this happens is called the *dew point*. If the air continues to rise further, the condensed water droplets will join together to form drops of rain. A shower, or perhaps even a thunderstorm, will be the result. This kind of rain is called *convectional rain*. The low density of the air also causes the *pressure* of the air to be low (Figure A, left). Low pressure pockets or 'cells' often bring cloudiness and rain.

The opposite of rising air is sinking or *subsiding* air. Cold air will be heavier and denser than the air around it and will sink. The pressure of subsiding air will be high (Figure A, right). Subsiding air cells often mean clear skies with few or no clouds, and normally bring dry weather.

Clouds, hills, and fronts

Clouds and rain can also occur in other ways. Figure B shows what happens when air which has picked up a lot of moisture over the sea is forced to rise over a range of hills. As it rises up the *windward* side of the hills it cools and forms clouds. If the air goes on rising there may be rain. Otherwise the clouds eventually break up. The air which descends the *leeward* side of the hills will be dry. Because this side of the hills receives no rain it is in a *rain shadow*. Rain produced in this way is called *relief rain*.

You may have noticed that oil always floats on water. Cold and warm air masses are the same. Where moving masses of cold and warm air meet, the warm air will rise on top of the cold air. A boundary or *front* develops between the two air masses. The warm air rising along the front may well produce cloud and *frontal rain*.

Figure A (*below left*) Rising and (*below right*) sinking air cells.

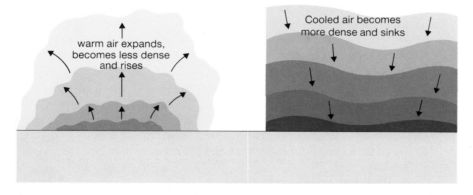

Figure B (*right*) How relief rain occurs

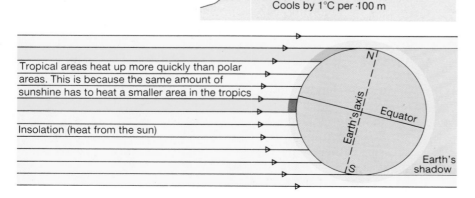

Figure C (*left*) Global heating by insolation

Figure D Fork lightning

Global patterns of air

On the world scale, air rises, sinks, and moves in the same sort of way described above. *Insolation* or radiation from the sun warms up the air of tropical regions much more than that of polar regions. The reason for this is that in polar regions the heating effect of the sun's rays on the ground surface is much more thinly spread (Figure C).

As cells of tropical air rise they turn into poleward flowing airstreams. An 'exchange' of air is set up, with warm tropical air flowing polewards and cold polar air moving towards the equator.

In reality the pattern of global air circulation is a lot more complicated. The rotation of the earth diverts airstreams to the right in the northern hemisphere, and to the left in the southern hemisphere. The distribution of continents and oceans also affects global airflow patterns. Some movements take place at high levels while others occur in the lower part of the atmosphere.

Figure E shows and names some of the main air cells, flows, and waves. The cells called depressions and anticyclones are directly responsible for a lot of our weather. All the cells and flows on the diagram are constantly changing even though the basic pattern remains the same.

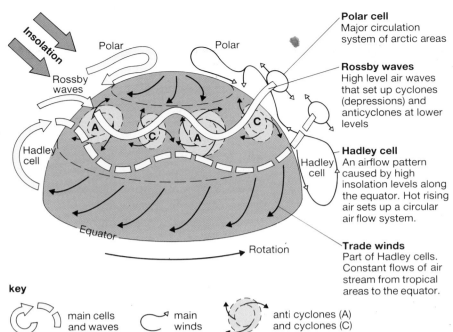

Polar cell
Major circulation system of arctic areas

Rossby waves
High level air waves that set up cyclones (depressions) and anticyclones at lower levels

Hadley cell
An airflow pattern caused by high insolation levels along the equator. Hot rising air sets up a circular air flow system.

Trade winds
Part of Hadley cells. Constant flows of air stream from tropical areas to the equator.

key

main cells and waves   main winds   anti cyclones (A) and cyclones (C)

Figure E The circulation of air in the Northern Hemisphere

QUESTIONS

1 Copy and complete this table:

Rising air	Subsiding air
?	Dense, heavy
At low pressure	?
May lead to clouds	?
?	Rain unlikely

   b) Give your table a suitable heading.

2 Write a definition of each of the following terms:
   a) convection   **d)** insolation
   b) rain shadow   **e)** front
   c) dew point

3 Write a paragraph explaining the differences between the following three types:
   a) convectional rain   **b)** frontal rain   **c)** relief rain

4 What information shows you that:
   a) the behaviour of air depends on its temperature
   b) global airflow depends on the earth's rotation
   c) without the sun there would be no weather

5 **a)** In your atlases find maps of the world showing pressure conditions in January and July. On a world map mark and label a suitable area of the world with this phrase:
   'Pressure is low all the year round'
   b) Repeat the exercise for three other areas using these phrases:
   i) 'Pressure stays high all the year'
   ii) 'Pressure is high in January but low in July'
   iii) 'Pressure is high in July but low in January'

Anticyclones

The weather conditions in Figures A and E were *both* brought about by subsiding cells of air. Subsiding cells that occur on a large scale (sometimes covering big areas of Europe) are called *anticyclones*. On a weather map an anticyclone is marked as *high* because it is an area of high pressure. Weather forecasters sometimes also talk about a 'ridge of high pressure'. This brings similar weather, although it does not usually last as long.

Anticyclones or ridges bring dry, clear weather. In winter, anticyclonic weather is often very cold, with frosty mornings and bright sunny periods during the day. Despite the sunshine the temperature may not rise much above freezing. Antifreeze is necessary for cars left out all night. In summer, anticyclones bring hot, sunny days, ideal for sunbathing. An established anticyclone often lasts for several days, so there is little variation in the weather. 'Heatwave' conditions can last for several weeks.

Depressions

The diary extracts in the panel were written by a student who was staying at a seaside resort. She recorded how the weather changed when a *depression* passed over the town. A depression is a low pressure cell where different sorts of air converge and tend to rise.

Diary extracts

The weather had been cold and dry for several days. On Thursday afternoon it became cloudier and the wind began to feel stronger. During the night we heard it raining, and on Friday morning it was quite a bit warmer. It was also cloudy, and drizzly to begin with.

There were some sunny periods during Friday morning, but by tea-time it was becoming cloudy and windy again. During the evening it rained very hard until well after bedtime.

On Saturday morning it was cold and gusty, and there were some showers. During the afternoon the clouds broke up and we had some sunny spells.

Figure A (*above*) A crowded Spanish beach in summer

Figure B (*right*) Formation and growth of a depression

Figure C (*below*) Cross-section through a depression

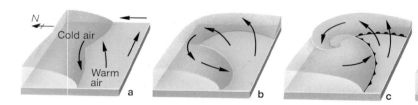

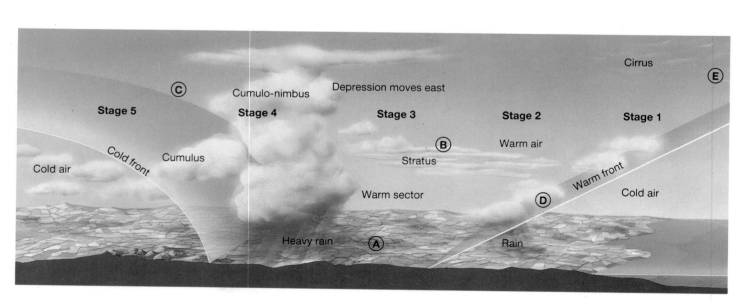

Figure B shows how a depression begins and then grows. It often starts where air from a warm anticyclone meets air from a cold anticyclone. The two sorts of air do not mix very well and a 'wave' develops along the boundary between them. This wave then bulges into a V-shape and becomes the centre of a low pressure cell. The two sides of the wave become cold and warm fronts. Eventually the cold front catches up with the warm front and the depression is 'occluded'. Fronts forming the wave move eastwards all the time.

Figure C is a cross-section through a depression at Stage C in Figure C, slicing through the two fronts. The entire system of fronts and clouds, together with the weather they bring, passed over the student at the seaside. Work out how the entries in the diary relate to the changing weather within the depression. Question 4 will help you.

Sometimes one depression follows on behind another. The weather will be variable, with short sunny spells giving way to longer periods of cloud and rain. Where these sorts of conditions occur in winter, it makes the weather quite mild. Depressional summers however are miserable, and we long for the hot sunny conditions brought by anticyclones.

Figure D Snow covered cars in winter

Wind

Sometimes wind can be the result of pressure differences between anticyclones and depressions, or perhaps between local high and low pressure cells. The rotation of the earth causes winds to spiral out of anticyclones and into depressions. Notice the circular wind pattern around the depression.

QUESTIONS

1 a) Describe *two* different sorts of weather which can be brought by anticyclones.
  b) What causes the differences?

2 a) Study the four diagrams showing how a depression develops. Which one do you think shows a 'mature' depression?
  b) Copy this diagram, clearly labelling the *warm sector*.

3 a) Study Figure B. Now make a copy of Figure C which shows the outline of the pattern of fronts.
  b) Match up the features **A–E** with these descriptions:
    i)   a front sloping at a gentle angle
    ii) a front which will force the air up quickly
    iii) somewhere with dry weather but expecting heavy rain
    iv) cloud in layers, not heaped
    v)   clouds so high they freeze

4 Study Figure C. Copy and complete the table below by filling in the boxes. The table has been started for you.

Stage	Sky	Cloud type	Rainfall	Cold/warm
1 Warm front approaches	Sunny but with high cloud			
2 Warm front passes				
3 Warm sector passes		Stratus		
4 Cold front approaches			Heavy rain	
5 After the cold front				Cold

5 'A trough of low pressure will move across the country this morning. During the afternoon the trough will clear. For the next two or three days the weather will be dominated by an anticyclone.'
  Write in as much detail as you can about the weather features likely to be experienced under these conditions. Draw attention to how pressure, winds, cloud, and rainfall might change.

The farmer's weather

Although modern farming uses a lot of machinery and technical know-how, the farmer still has to take the weather into account. Unexpected weather can upset even the best of farming plans.

Some crops cannot be sown or planted out too early in the year, otherwise the young plants will be damaged by spring frosts. Potatoes for example are not planted out until March. The farmer is therefore interested in the *frost-free period*, which is the number of months in the year when frost does not occur.

For most plants no growth at all takes place unless the temperature is at least 6° C. On a chilly day in winter this may only happen for about two or three hours a day, if at all. The number of months in the year when the temperature is above 6° C is called the *growing season*.

The farmer learns by experience which parts of his farm are likely to be the coldest. He will avoid planting tender crops on valley bottoms which collect heavy, frosty air that drains down the slopes. Vine growers in France and other wine-producing areas plant their vines on south-facing slopes to avoid frost and to get the most sunshine. In eastern England, shelter belts of trees will help to keep the worst of the weather off the young cereal crops. The same areas are likely to have long, sunny days in summer when the crop is ripening.

Market gardeners need to have their crops ready as early as possible in the year, when demand and prices are high. Often they can achieve this only by creating their own weather inside greenhouses made of glass or polythene. Here artificial heat can be used to keep the crops at just the right temperature.

Farmers are also concerned about the moisture needs of crops. In many climates no farming at all is possible without irrigation. Figure A shows an area where irrigation is used to increase yields. Crops may also have too much moisture. Wheat is often unsuccessful in damper areas of Britain. A wet summer is a problem for all farmers, since heavy rainfall flattens crops and makes them difficult to harvest.

Figure A (*top*) Giant irrigation systems in the Kufra desert of Libya

Figure B (*bottom*) How land and sea breezes develop

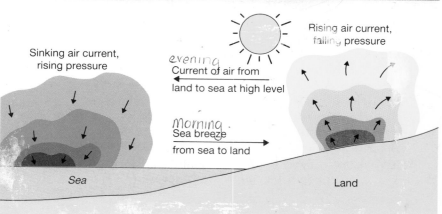

Sinking air current, rising pressure

Rising air current, falling pressure

evening
Current of air from land to sea at high level

Morning
Sea breeze from sea to land

Sea

Land

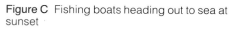
Figure C Fishing boats heading out to sea at sunset

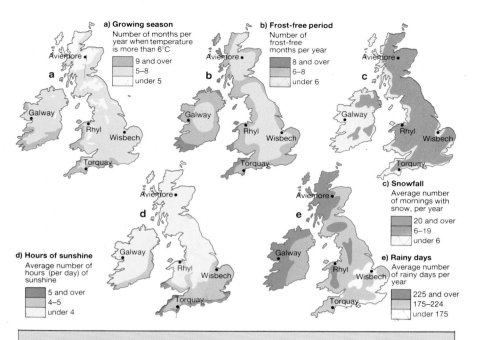

Figure D a) The growing season, b) The frost-free period, c) Snow records, d) Sunshine records, e) Rainy days

a) Growing season
Number of months per year when temperature is more than 6°C
- 9 and over
- 5–8
- under 5

b) Frost-free period
Number of frost-free months per year
- 8 and over
- 6–8
- under 6

c) Snowfall
Average number of mornings with snow, per year
- 20 and over
- 6–19
- under 6

d) Hours of sunshine
Average number of hours (per day) of sunshine
- 5 and over
- 4–5
- under 4

e) Rainy days
Average number of rainy days per year
- 225 and over
- 175–224
- under 175

Weather at the seaside

'We had a lovely time at the seaside. Back home everyone said it had rained all day.'

'It was quite warm at home. But when we reached the coast, it was too cold to sit on the beach. We needed our jumpers.'

Coastal places sometimes seem to have weather all of their own. Land and sea breezes sometimes explain this. These are local winds set up by differences in heating between land and sea (Figure B). During the day, land surfaces will heat up more quickly than the water. Rising currents of warm, buoyant air will develop. As the air parcels expand and rise, their pressure falls. The pressure difference between sea and land causes air to be drawn in across the coastline. On the beach we feel this as a cool, gentle *sea breeze*. At night the reverse happens. The land loses heat faster than the sea, and subsiding or sinking air parcels develop over the land. Their pressure is high compared with the sea air, and so the wind blows the other way. This is a *land breeze*.

Coastal fishermen know how to make use of land and sea breezes. The land breeze blows the fishing boat gently out to sea during the evening (Figure C). In the morning it will be blown back towards the shore by the sea breeze.

The sunshine map (Figure D) shows that many coastal places have more sunshine than places further inland. This of course helps to explain the popularity of seaside places as holiday resorts. A hot day is not much use for sunbathing if the weather remains overcast and muggy, and the sun hardly ever comes out. Figure C on page 86 helps to explain why coastal places often get less rain and more sunshine than inland places.

QUESTIONS

1 What is meant by the following:
   a) frost-free period?   b) growing season?

2 Describe how each of the following farmers deals with the problem of frost:
   a) potato grower
   b) vine grower in France
   c) farmer in eastern England

3 Figure B shows how a sea breeze develops. Draw a similar diagram to explain a *land breeze*. Label it in the same way.

4 a) Using your atlases, name the *country* and *county* (or region) of the five places shown in Figure D.
   b) Using the maps in Figure D write down:
      i)   how much sunshine Torquay can expect each year
      ii) how much snow Aviemore might expect
      iii) how much frost Rhyl might expect
      iv) how Galway compares with the rest of Ireland for rainy days
      v)   how the growing season for Wisbech compares with the rest of England.
   c) What factors help to explain:
      i)   why Torquay and Rhyl are popular holiday resorts
      ii) why Aviemore is a popular winter resort
      iii) why arable farming and market gardening are more important than grass and livestock around Wisbech
      iv) why grass for livestock farming grows well around Galway.
   d) What factors help to explain:
      i)   why early potatoes are unlikely to be grown near Wisbech but might be grown near Galway
      ii) why Torquay might get more winter visitors than Rhyl.

5 'Coastal places seem to have weather all of their own.' From the information shown on this page, do you agree with this? Give reasons.

8.6 Town weather

Figure A shows temperature readings taken at various points around the buildings and grounds of a school. The points were carefully located so that they were evenly spaced, and the readings were all carried out by pupils at the same time. The geography teacher then drew the map opposite to show how the temperature varied between the points. Complete question 1 now, before you go on reading.

Notice how the school buildings themselves and the areas close to them are noticeably warmer than the areas further away. The school is like an island of warmth surrounded by colder air. This is why the pattern formed is called a *heat island*.

Studying heat islands

Heat islands don't just occur around single buildings. They also occur around entire towns and cities. Figure B shows London's heat island. The temperature readings shown were taken on a night in October. Notice how the heat island is roughly the same shape as the built-up area.

Causes of heat islands

Heat islands occur for a number of reasons:

● Man-made surfaces like bricks, tarmac, and concrete store up heat from the sun during the day and release it at night.

● Homes, factories, and other buildings heat up during the day. They stay warm for a long time at night even though the temperature outside falls.

● The haze and dust in the air above cities reflects back much of the heat generated by buildings.

The heat island effect also influences other aspects of the climates of towns. Compare the humidity map in Figure A with your coloured-in map for question 1. Where are the temperatures highest? Where is humidity highest? Notice that warmer places experience noticeably lower humidity.

Wind in towns

Around tall buildings the wind can often be very blustery, even on a day when there seems to be little wind elsewhere. If you try to work out where the wind is coming from, you find that it varies constantly in direction and speed.

Figure A Temperature and humidity readings taken around a school (see question 1)

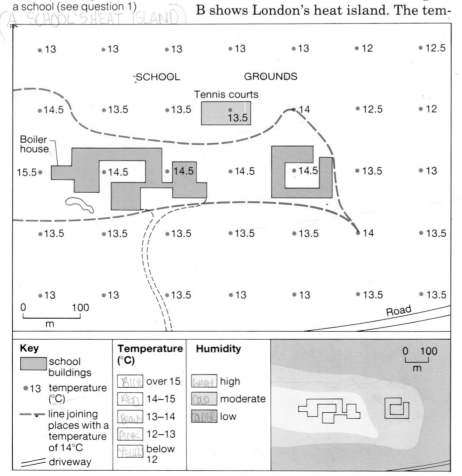

Figure B London's heat island one night in May

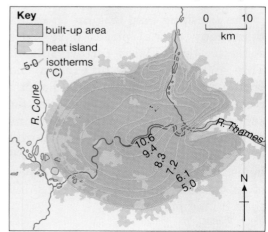

Towns generate their own wind patterns. Rows of tall buildings act as 'funnels' for air, channelling it in particular directions and making it move more quickly. Miniature heat islands around buildings also cause differences in air density and pressure. These cause further air movements and contribute to the gusty conditions. Urban winds extend upwards to several hundred metres. Only above this height do the 'normal' winds of the weather forecast begin to take over.

Urban climates

There are several other ways in which the climates of towns and cities differ from those of the surrounding countryside. Figure C shows some of these. Although towns are warmer than the countryside, they are often not as sunny. One reason for this is that the urban atmosphere contains more pollutants like sulphur dioxide and carbon monoxide. These form a haze which scatters some of the incoming sunshine. These pollutants also encourage condensation to occur more readily, so that urban places have more rain than the countryside. In particular, pollutants in the urban atmosphere cause a great deal more fog. The problem of fog in cities and along urban roads and motorways is looked at on the next page.

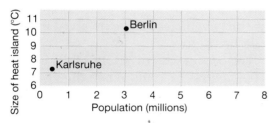

City	Population (millions)	Size of heat island (°C)
Karlsruhe	0.3	7.1
Malmo	0.5	7.4
Utrecht	0.5	6.0
Sheffield	0.5	8.0
Munich	1.3	7.1
Vienna	1.9	8.1
Berlin	3.1	10.2
London	7.2	10.0

Figure D Data and graph for question 2

Figure C How urban climates differ from nearby rural climates

Feature of climate or atmosphere	Amount by which urban places differ from rural places
Sulphur dioxide content	× 200
Carbon monoxide content	× 200
Dust particles	× 5
Insolation (solar heat)	− 15 to 20%
Sunshine hours	− 5 to 15%
Winter minimum temperature	+ 1°C to 2°C
Average wind speed	− 20 to 30%
Winter fog	+ 100%
Summer fog	+ 30%
Cloud	+ 5 to 10%
Total rainfall	+ 5 to 10%

QUESTIONS

1 a) Make a copy of Figure A on tracing paper. Write in the temperature figures neatly and carefully.
b) Notice the line which forms a loop. It joins points which have a temperature of 14°C. It encloses all points which have a temperature above 14°C, leaving points with a lower temperature on the outside. Work out how the teacher drew this line.
c) Now draw similar lines for 12°C, 13°C and 15°C.
d) Using a suitable colour scheme complete the key and colour in your map. Give your map a title.
e) Describe the pattern made by the shadings. Can you explain it?

2 a) Draw an enlarged copy of the graph in Figure D and complete it using the data supplied. The temperature data shows the size of heat islands for different cities – that is, the temperature difference between the city and its surrounding countryside.
b) 'Bigger cities have bigger heat islands.' From your graph do you think this is true?

3 Copy out this extract and fill in the blank spaces:
'The urban atmosphere contains about —————— times more sulphur dioxide than the atmosphere of the countryside. Cities have ————— sunshine than rural places but still have —————— temperatures. If you live in a town you can expect to get about —————— per cent more rain than if you live in the country and about —————— per cent more fog in the winter.'

4 Look at the map of London's heat island (Figure B). Suggest why:
a) temperatures were low along lower Thameside
b) temperatures were high over the West End
c) the heat island effect would have been more marked at 4 a.m. than at 11 p.m.

5 Compare the pattern of humidity around the school with the temperature pattern (Figure A). Can you explain the similarities and differences?

6 From previous pages, describe how any *three* of the conditions mentioned in Figure C could be measured.

7 'Country places get better weather than towns.' Do you agree with this? Give reasons for your answer.

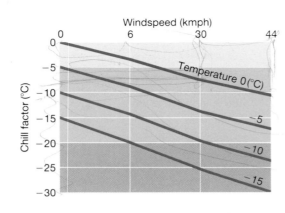

Figure A A wind-chill chart

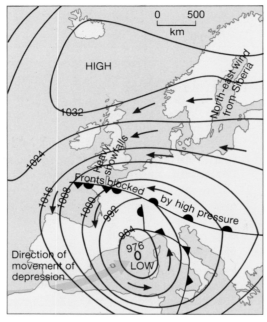

Figure B (*right*) The mixing of moist Atlantic air and cold Arctic air produced heavy snowfalls in January 1987

Figure C (*below*) The aftermath of an accident during heavy fog on the M1

Windy days in winter often seem particularly cold. In open areas a biting wind will make being out of doors especially unpleasant. Any sheltered spot out of the wind always seems much warmer. This is the result of the *wind-chill* effect, by which the wind causes the body to lose heat faster than it would do otherwise. The same effect can also be felt where the body is moving through still air. Motorcyclists often need to wear warm clothes even when pedestrians are wearing much less. The effect can however be turned to advantage. The air which makes the motorcyclist feel chilled will also cool his motorcycle's engine. A wind-chill chart is shown with the weather meter on page 82. Another one is shown in Figure A as a graph. On the graph a wind speed of 30 km per hour will make a temperature of 0° C feel like −6° C.

Ice and snow bring particular hazards for travellers. The weather map (Figure B) shows conditions in January 1987. Fronts carrying moist air from the Atlantic met bitterly cold streams of air from northern Europe. The heavy snowfall brought road and rail transport in some areas to a standstill.

The fog hazard

News bulletins often contain reports of multiple crashes or pile-ups on motorways caused by fog. As many as twenty or thirty vehicles can be involved in one pile-up (Figure C).

Fog occurs when visibility falls below 1 000 metres or 1 km. When the visibility falls below 200 metres we call it thick fog. (On average this happens on five days a year in Britain.) Fog consists of water vapour which has condensed to form tiny water droplets in the air. There are different sorts of fog. *Hill fog* is simply low cloud, but can be as hazardous as proper fog in hilly areas. Figure D describes three other kinds of fog: *advection fog*, *steam fog* and *radiation fog*.

Polluted fog

In towns and cities the fog problem is made worse by atmospheric pollution. Soot and sulphur dioxide from chimneys turn fog into deadly *smog*. In London in December 1952, four thousand people died from bronchitis and pneumonia caused by smog. Since then clean air laws have cleaned much of the soot from the air of cities. A problem which has appeared since however is *photochemical smog*. This is caused by sunlight turning car exhaust fumes into a foul yellow haze. Besides being a health hazard it reduces visibility and contributes to traffic problems. In many cities, such as Los Angeles, it never really goes away.

Problems for flying

Snow, ice, and fog cause some of their biggest problems at airports. Airports sometimes have to close for several hours or even days because of ice on the runways or fog. Fog or mist can make take-off hazardous. At Tenerife airport in the Canary Islands in 1977 two jumbo jets collided as they were taking off, killing 547 people. Because it was misty and drizzling the air traffic controllers failed to notice that one aircraft was taxiing into the path of the other. The extract (Figure E) describes an air accident in New York.

Figure E An air disaster in New York, USA

On 28 July 1945 a United States bomber pilot, completely blinded by a New York fog, crashed into the Empire State Building, killing fifteen people. The plane crashed into the seventy-ninth floor. The top of the fog bank was a mere 5 metres (16 feet) above the point of the accident so that the top few floors of the skyscraper were bathed in sunshine at the time.

From *Disasters* by John Whittow

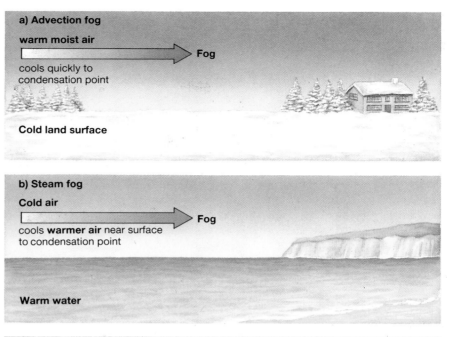

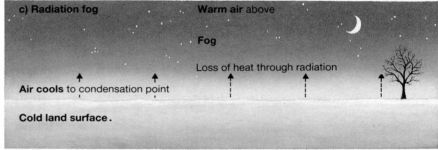

Figure D Types of fog

QUESTIONS

1 Using the wind-chill chart (Figure A), work out the temperature that will be felt by:
   a) a motor-cyclist travelling at 44 kph on a frosty day when a thermometer inside a Stevenson Screen (p. 82) reads −5°C.
   b) a pupil taking weather recordings from a Stevenson Screen in a wind of 30 kph when a thermometer inside the Screen reads 0°C.

2 Describe *three* ways in which you might notice the cooling effect of the wind.

3 Which type of fog are you likely to drive into:
   a) in the hills on a cloudy day?
   b) going to school on a November morning?
   c) along the coast?
   d) after a snowy period?

4 Describe and explain *three* ways in which travellers may be affected by fog.

5 Read the extract about the air disaster at New York in 1945 (Figure E). Draw a sketch to illustrate the situation. On the sketch provide labels to explain why the top floors of the skyscraper might have been free of fog.

Unit 8 ASSESSMENT

The weather forecast – how correct?

We sometimes wonder how accurate the weather forecast really is. This assessment unit will help you to decide if the weather forecasters get it right or not. If they are wrong, how wrong are they? Are some parts of the weather forecast more accurate than others?

Stage 1

Study Figure A which shows the weather forecast provided by a national newspaper in July 1989.

1 Copy out and complete this description of the weather situation:
   At noon on Friday 14th July pressure is expected to be ... over Southern Britain, about ... millibars. A ... front lies off the west coast of Ireland, while a warm front lies across ... These fronts are part of a depression which is centred out in the Atlantic to the south of ...
   (5 marks)

2 Which part of Britain is likely to have:
   a) the highest temperature on Friday afternoon?
   b) the lowest temperature on Friday evening?
   c) sunny periods on Friday morning?
   d) fog on hills on Friday?
   e) very rough seas on Friday evening? (5 marks)

3 Explain what is meant on the weather map by:
   a) the term *high*
   b) the term *trough*
   c) the joining together of the two symbols for *fronts*
   (5 marks)

Stage 2

The following day (Saturday) the same newspaper published a list of places in Britain and the weather conditions they had actually experienced. The data for some of these places is summarised in Figure B.

4 On an outline map of Britain locate the places named in Figure B. For each place draw a symbol to represent the actual weather, using the data from the table. Follow the symbols used in TV weather reports. These are on page 80. You may need to add descriptive words if no symbol is available. Remember to provide a key to your map.
   (15 marks)

Figure A Newspaper weather forecast for Saturday 15 July

5 Below your map write a paragraph describing how the weather varied across Britain. In your work you should draw attention to:
   a) where the warmest and coolest parts of the country were
   b) where the brightest and cloudiest parts were
   c) where the wettest and driest parts were.   (10 marks)

FIGURE A

WEATHER: GENERAL OUTLOOK
Weather forecast for 6 am to midnight today (14/7/89)
General situation: A warm front will move slowly across the British Isles.

Northern Ireland, Scotland, North Wales, northern and central England will start cloudy with outbreaks of mainly light rain or drizzle, though some of this may be heavy in Scotland and northern England at first, with fog on hills and along the coasts. This will gradually be replaced in Northern Ireland and the West by bright showery weather.

Southern England, the Midlands and South Wales will start cloudy but should stay mainly dry. There will be some bright or sunny spells though, especially in south east England.

Temperatures will remain near normal but warm in sunnier southern locations.

Outlook for the following 48 hours: Remaining generally unsettled with rain or drizzle in the North and West with temperatures near normal, but warmer and drier with sunny spells in the South.

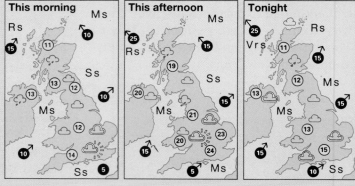

Key
M s Moderate sea
S s Smooth sea
R s Rough sea
V r s Very rough sea

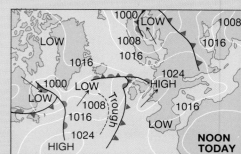

Figure B Weather readings for Saturday 11 July

Place	Sunshine (hrs)	Rain (ins)	Maximum temperature °C	Weather
Wick	2.9	0.16	11	rain
Stornoway	0.3	0.06	13	rain
Glasgow	—	0.65	19	rain
Belfast	0.3	0.44	22	showers
Blackpool	0.6	0.46	20	showers
Manchester	0.5	0.09	22	drizzle
Cardiff	4.0	—	24	sunny
Scarborough	4.9	0.14	22	bright
Cromer	2.0	—	25	bright
Norwich	3.7	0.2	25	cloudy
London	4.0	—	27	bright
Penzance	8.4	—	21	sunny

Stage 3

Finally, compare your actual weather map with the weather forecaster's predictions. Summarise the comparison by copying and completing Figure C.

From your table say how accurate you think the forecast was. Would any places have found it unreliable? (20 marks)

Total: 60 marks

Figure C Summary of actual weather compared with the forecast

Region	Ways in which the forecast was right	Ways in which the forecast was wrong
Wick, Stornoway, and N. Scotland		
Glasgow and S. Scotland		
Belfast and N. Ireland		
Blackpool, Cardiff, Manchester, west coast, Wales		
Scarborough, Cromer, Norwich, east coast		
London, SE England		
Penzance, SW England		

Details for pupil profile sheets Unit 8

Knowledge and understanding

1 Techniques of weather forecasting
2 Weather map symbols
3 Processes in the atmosphere: insolation, convection, subsidence, winds, fog, condensation, cloud formation, rain
4 Processes and features of: anticyclones, depressions, fronts, urban heat islands, urban climates

Skills

1 Measurement of weather conditions from instruments and presentation of results
2 Interpretation of cloud patterns from satellite photographs
3 Interpretation of TV and newspaper weather reports
4 Interpretation of climatic maps
5 Drawing weather maps from data
6 Drawing isotherm maps from data

Values

1 Awareness of how different groups of people are dependent on the weather – eg. farmers, tourists
2 Awareness of peoples' attitudes towards the reliability of the weather forecast

Unit 9: Climate around the world

Figure A shows some climatic data for Denver, Colorado, USA. Notice the different types of information shown in the table. The data can be presented as a *climatic graph*. Monthly temperature and rainfall are shown on separate vertical axes. Temperature values are shown as a continuous line, while rainfall is shown in a bar graph beneath. Annual temperature range and annual rainfall total are often printed above the graph. Most climatic graphs are drawn in this or a similar way. Climatic graphs for different places can then be compared easily.

Temperate climates

The graph for Denver has several features which characterize a *temperate* climate. There are only a few months of the year in which the average temperature falls below 6°C, which is the minimum for plant growth. This means that there is a long growing season that can support a wide range of crops. On the other hand the climate only becomes hot in the summer. In the northern hemisphere, summer is in June, July, and August. If Denver was in the southern hemisphere the warmest months would be November, December, and January. There is also a marked seasonality in the climate, that is, the temperature difference between the warmest and coldest months ranges over several degrees.

Besides being temperate, the climate of Denver is also *continental* in character. Cold, dry winters contrast with hot thundery summers. Because it is in the middle of the American continent, the Denver area warms up much more quickly in summer than coastal regions do. It also cools down very quickly in winter, so that the seasonal differences in temperature are very high. Rainfall totals are low, and most of the rain falls during early summer thunderstorms. This means that a lot of moisture is lost by evaporation, and that the amount of rain which is available for crop growth is even less.

Figure A Location and climate of Denver, Colorado

Climatic data for Denver, Colorado, USA
Altitude 1613 m
Range 23°C

	J	F	M	A	M	J	J	A	S	O	N	D	Year
Temperature (°C)	0	2	5	8	14	20	22	21	16	11	4	−1	10°C (average)
Rainfall (mm)	18	20	25	49	58	28	45	27	24	24	12	24	304 mm (total)

Location of Denver

Denver

Line of transect

Climate graph for Denver, Colorado, USA

Total rainfall 304 mm

Range 23°C

Temperature (°C)

Rainfall (mm)

J F M A M J J A S O N D

Horizontal scale

0   400

km

Height (m)

Rocky Mountains

Denver

Mississippi River

Figure B A tornado on the Great Plains

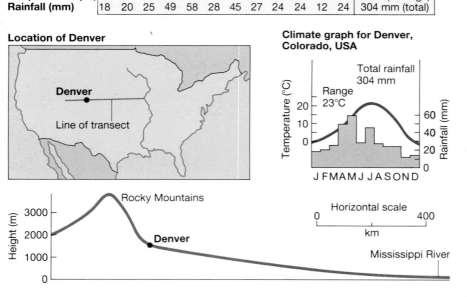

The Great Plains

Denver is on the Great Plains of North America, between the Rocky Mountains and the basin of the Mississippi (Figure A). The height of the Plains, at 1600 metres, adds to the extremes of climate. Summer days are hot and dry, while in the winter the Plains are swept by snowstorms, frosts, and blizzards. Rainfall totals and the reliability of the rainfall both decrease westwards towards the foothills of the Rockies.

Before the coming of white people, the Plains were areas of grassland or 'prairies' where Indians lived and hunted wild buffalo. The first white settlers drove the Indians from the Plains and used the grasses for cattle grazing.

Farmers from the wetter east of America then ploughed up the prairies for wheat growing. The wheat farmers moved on to the Plains during a period of relatively wet years. This led them to think that the climate of the Plains was always wet – in other words, that they were experiencing average conditions. At first their wheat farming was very successful, but by the 1930s rainfall levels were well below average. A succession of drought years turned the Plains from a grain farming area into a huge 'Dust Bowl'. The bare soil was rapidly eroded by wind and tornadoes (see Figures B and C) which ruined the Plains for cultivation for many years to come. Thousands of farmers had to leave their homes and migrate to other parts of the United States.

Climatic averages

The Dust Bowl example shows the usefulness and the problems of climatic data based on averages. It is much more important for farmers to know how reliable rainfall is, that is, how much it varies from year to year, than it is to know the average rainfall. Figure D shows the years when wheat growing on the Plains would have been unsuccessful.

Figure C Dust storm near Panhandle on the Great Plains in the 1930s

QUESTIONS

1 Name *four* sorts of information which you ought to be able to obtain from a climatic graph.

2 List and describe the climatic hazards which farmers on the Great Plains are likely to experience.

3 Use the data below to answer the following questions.
   Climatic data for Christchurch, New Zealand

Altitude	10 m			Range	10° C								
	J	F	M	A	M	J	J	A	S	O	N	D	Year
T (°C)	16	16	14	12	9	6	6	7	9	12	14	16	11
P (mm)	56	43	48	48	66	66	69	48	46	43	48	56	638

   a) Draw a climatic graph from the data like the one for Denver.
   b) Name *two* features of the graph which show you that it relates to a temperate area.
   c) Name *two* ways in which the climate of Christchurch is different from that of Denver.
   d) Christchurch has a coastal location. How do you think this may affect the differences you have noted in c)?

4 Study the graph (Figure D) for Oklahoma, another city on the Great Plains.
   a) In which year would farmers have been likely to be doing well?
   b) In which years would they have been likely to be doing very badly?
   c) When might farmers have been likely to have started to move back into the Plains?

5 'Unreliable rainfall is worse than low rainfall'. Do you agree? Give reasons for your answer.

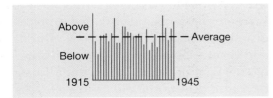

Figure D Rainfall data for Oklahoma over a thirty-year period

9.2 Desertification: the Sahel

Figure A Cattle at a well in the Sahel region of Mauritania

Figure B Montly rainfall figures over a five-year period for Agades, Niger

Month	Rainfall in mm				
	Year 1	Year 2	Year 3	Year 4	Year 5
January	—		—	—	—
February	—	—	—	—	—
March	—	2	—	—	—
April	—	—	50	—	—
May	22	—	1	18	—
June	7	2	20	1	—
July	11	58	61	9	22
August	36	67	26	51	14
September	21	26	8	3	4
October	—	—	—	—	—
November	—	—	—	—	—
December	—	—	—	—	—
Total	97	155	166	82	40

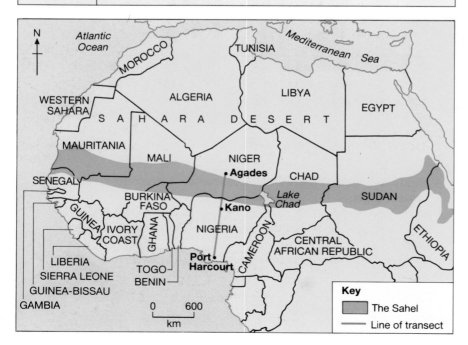

Figure C The countries of the Sahel (see Figure D for transect)

As you travel northwards on the road from Tahoua, the landscape becomes sandier and the vegetation sparse. The wind blows stronger from the north-east, and the air is often full of sand and dust picked off the arid, deforested land. Sandstorms are a commonplace in the dry season as the rains are eagerly awaited. This is the Sahel belt of West Africa.

Study Figure B. It shows rainfall figures for Agades, a town in the state of Niger in the southern Sahara, 450 km north east of Tahoua. Answer Question 1 before you read on.

The Sahel

Agades lies on the northern edge of the Sahel (see Figure C). The Sahel is the southern fringe of the Sahara. It is a *transitional zone* between the *savanna* lands which lie to the south and the Sahara desert to the north. It has some of the features of both areas.

Like the Sahara, the Sahel has very little rainfall. This is because it experiences dry winds all the year round. In the winter these winds blow off the Sahara from the north-east. In summer the area receives southerly winds which cross the coast of West Africa, but these are dry by the time they reach the Sahel. You can see that even the small amounts of rain received at Agades vary considerably from year to year.

Further south, rainfall totals increase, and so does the reliability of the rainfall. With the increase in rainfall the vegetation changes from desert types to savanna (also called tropical grassland). Figure D shows how rainfall and vegetation are related to each other in this part of Africa. The rainfall pattern also affects the *runoff regime* (see pages 44–45) of rivers.

Desertification

Since 1968 rainfall in the Sahel has been well below average. This has meant that with less moisture available for plant growth, the quality of the grassland has deteriorated, and more bare soil has become exposed to the sun and dry winds. As a result soil erosion by the wind has increased. This in turn has meant that grazing land has been destroyed. The desert margin has gradually moved southwards into the Sahel. This advance of the desert at the expense of the savanna is called *desertification*. It is a major environmental problem worldwide. You can find out more about how big the problem is on p. 122. Geographers and scientists now understand that people contribute as much to desertification as nature does.

In the countries of the Sahel, better medical care over the last thirty years has caused death rates to fall. As a result populations are steadily increasing. Many peoples of the Sahel are nomadic herders, so more livestock has been needed to support the growing population. This has caused overgrazing of pastures, and contributed to more soil erosion.

The effects of desertification have been very far reaching. Some herders have lost their herds in the drought. Others have given up their nomadic way of life and become farmers. This has put pressure on land in damper, more settled parts of the Sahel, leading to overcultivation and further soil erosion. Many people have abandoned their traditional ways of life entirely and gone to live in towns.

In 1984–5 these conditions produced famine on a huge scale in Ethiopia. The famine attracted international attention. Many people remember the raising of funds for this famine through a series of worldwide rock concerts called 'Live Aid'. Now, years later, conditions are still desperate in the area.

Latitude (°N)	Agades (17)		Kano (12 30)		Port Harcourt (4 40)
	20	15	10		5
Rainfall totals	under 250 mm		750 mm		2000 mm
Rainfall reliability	very unreliable		fairly unreliable		reliable
Length of rainy season (months)	1–2				10–12
Vegetation	desert types	short grass	long grass scattered trees		rain forest coastal mangrove forest

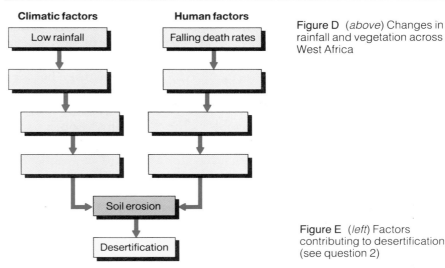

Figure D (*above*) Changes in rainfall and vegetation across West Africa

Figure E (*left*) Factors contributing to desertification (see question 2)

QUESTIONS

1 **a)** Find Agades in an atlas. State its latitude and longitude.

b) Your atlas probably shows that Agades is on a motor road that crosses the Sahara from Kano in Niger to In Salah and Algiers in Algeria. How far is Agades from:
    i) The nearest place southwards along the road?
    ii) In Salah?

c) Draw a graph to show rainfall totals in Agades for the five-year period shown in Figure B.

d) Calculate the average rainfall for the period. Show this rainfall on your graph by a horizontal line.

e) Suggest why the 'average rainfall' line is not very meaningful.

f) In which months could Agades people be sure of some rain?

g) In which months would Agades people be most uncertain about rainfall?

2 Copy out and complete Figure E. Give it the heading 'Factors contributing to desertification in the Sahel'.

3 Describe *three* ways in which the nomadic peoples are responding to the problem of desertification.

4 Look back at the information on desert landscapes on pages 28 and 29. Describe how the landscape would change on a journey northwards from Agades. Explain the changes you describe by referring to the climate and the processes which are affecting the landscape.

Some places always seem to be suffering from one sort of natural disaster or another. Bangladesh is one of the world's poorest and most densely populated countries, but is often in the news because of disasters brought about by drought or flood.

Bangladesh's problems arise partly out of its *monsoonal* pattern of climate. The climatic graph for Dhaka (Figure A) shows the features of a monsoon climate. The year can be divided into three main seasons. From November to February there is a 'cool dry' season with mild temperatures and hardly any rain. March to May is the 'hot dry' season, when the weather becomes very warm but is still dry. Late May to October is the monsoon season, a period of heavy, almost continuous rain which reaches a climax in July or August and gradually dies away in the autumn.

All countries in eastern Asia experience the monsoon to some extent, but its strength and timing varies. Shanghai in China lies further north, so its winter dry season is very much colder. At Madras in India the wettest time of the year is later than Dhaka, in September or October.

Causes of the monsoon

The monsoon is caused by global variations in rates of heating and cooling (Figure B). Warm, moist air is sucked across the Equator into the interior of Asia, bringing torrential rainfall to most parts of eastern Asia, especially coastal regions.

A feature of the monsoon season is its sudden arrival. For several days beforehand, the air will have been hot and very humid. Then the monsoon suddenly breaks, starting a period of rainfall which lasts for several weeks. Unfortunately the timing and the intensity of the monsoon are not reliable. In some years it can arrive several weeks late, and sometimes it has been known not to arrive at all.

The monsoon is critical to the people of Bangladesh and other eastern Asian countries. Most people are subsistence farmers, heavily dependent upon the success of their rice crop. Rice requires the flooded fields which the monsoon produces. If the monsoon is late or poor, starvation usually follows.

In winter the reverse climatic conditions develop (Figure C). A 'cold monsoon' of outblowing winds. These winds cross the Equator and give a hot, wet monsoon to the coastlands of northern Australia.

Typhoons

Bangladesh is also in the path of *typhoons* or 'tropical cyclones' (Figure D). These are intense storms likely to develop in all tropical seas. In the Caribbean area they are known as *hurricanes*. Typhoons have some of the

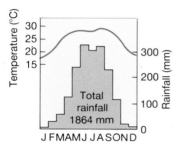

Figure A Climatic data for Dhaka

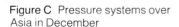

Figure B Pressure systems over Asia in July

Figure C Pressure systems over Asia in December

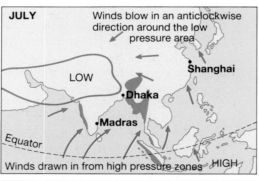

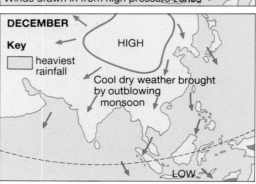

Figure D The paths of typhoons over south-east Asia

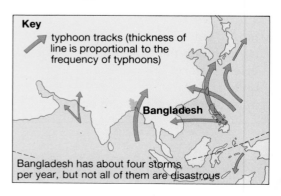

features of temperate depressions but are very much more powerful and highly destructive. They begin as upward currents of warm, moist air over the tropical oceans. As they move they develop into intense swirling masses of air and clouds with the following features:

- an upward spiralling vortex or corkscrew structure, sucking in hot, moist air from beneath. The winds inside can reach 270 km per hour.

- a central core or 'eye' about 20 km in diameter, with light winds and cloudless skies

- outside the eye the storm extends outwards for up to 150 km

- once generated it lasts several days, even weeks, and can cover thousands of miles

- especially destructive when it crosses coastlines, bringing huge tidal waves

- soon declines on reaching land, since there is no more hot, moist air to keep it going.

A typhoon hit Bangladesh in December 1988. The typhoon brought a tidal wave which flooded the coastlands, most of which is made up of low-lying islands. Newspapers reported 700 people dead and 300 000 homeless. The area was still recovering from further disastrous floods from August and September, and also from 1987. The government had been developing a disaster early warning system. 'We now know the cyclone didn't wait for us', a spokesman said.

Figure F Aftermath of a typhoon in Bangladesh

Figure E Cross section through a typhoon

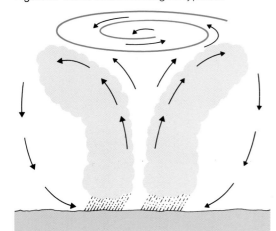

QUESTIONS

1 Study the climatic graph for Dhaka (Figure A).
  a) What is the temperature in May?
  b) What amount of rainfall can be expected in October?
  c) What is the annual range of temperature?
  d) How does the annual range of temperature compare with Denver (page 96)?
  e) How might Dhaka's temperatures be different if it had a mountain location?
  f) What months in Dhaka make up the monsoon (rainy) season?
  g) Approximately what proportion of Dhaka's rain comes in the monsoon season?
  h) During what months would you expect winds at Dhaka to be offshore?

2 From the text and figures:
  a) What has been the cause of the Bangladesh disaster?
  b) How have people been affected by it?

3 From Figure C and your atlases, name an area or country which:
  a) has high pressure in December
  b) has onshore winds in August
  c) has heavy rainfall in January
  d) receives many typhoons, other than Bangladesh.

4 Copy Figure E. Complete the diagram by adding labels to describe and explain the different features.

5 Reread the sections of this book about depressions (pp 86–87).
  a) find *two* similarities between depressions and typhoons.
  b) Find *four* differences between them.

6 'In Bangladesh the monsoon is more of a climatic problem than typhoons.' Do you agree or disagree with this view? Give reasons.

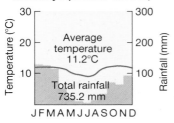

Lima (altitude 137 m)

Average temperature 18.0°C

Total rainfall 25.8 mm

J F M A M J J A S O N D

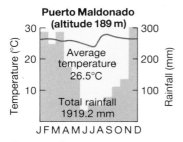

Huancayo (altitude 3379 m)

Average temperature 11.2°C

Total rainfall 735.2 mm

J F M A M J J A S O N D

Puerto Maldonado (altitude 189 m)

Average temperature 26.5°C

Total rainfall 1919.2 mm

J F M A M J J A S O N D

Figure A Climate graphs for Peruvian locations

Figure B (*left*) Fertile river mouth with Peruvian coastal desert in the background

Look at the climate graph for Lima (Figure A, top), the capital city of Peru. Lima is close to the coast and could be expected to receive good rainfall. But in this area, offshore winds blow all the year round. These bring no rain – Lima and the coastlands of Peru are deserts (Figure B).

Lima is only 12° south of the Equator. We might expect the climate to be hot for much of the year, but it is cooler than Puerto Maldonado (Figure A, bottom) which is at the same latitude, but in the interior. The reason for the lower temperatures of the Peruvian coast is the effect of the *Humboldt current*. This is an ocean current which carries cool water from the South Pacific and Antarctic areas towards the Equator. Like winds, ocean currents are a way in which heat is redistributed around the globe. Winds and sea breezes blowing over this current are cooled by it.

Altitude and vegetation

Temperatures decrease on average by about 1°C for every 100 metre increase in height. Much of Peru lies within the Andes, mountains which reach up to over 6000 m. This means that there are many places in Peru which are much cooler than Lima. For example Huancayo in the heart of the Peruvian Andes (see Figure A, middle). Answer question 1 before continuing.

The Andes cause a zoning of climate and vegetation with altitude. Figure C shows how the zones change from west to east across Peru. Notice that on the eastern side of the Andes the zones are different. The eastern foothills of the Andes form the western edge of the Amazon rainforests. Besides the main changes in vegetation shown in Figure C there are many localized variations. Leeward slopes (those facing away from the wind) have much less rain than windward slopes. Because of this localized *rain shadow* effect leeward slopes may be able to support only poor grass or scrub while nearby windward slopes are forested.

Altitude and people

The effects of altitude on climate are important for the people of the Peruvian Andes.

• The cooling effect of altitude makes life and work more comfortable than in low-lying tropical areas.

• A greater range of crops can be grown than would be possible in temperate regions at the same altitude. The height of the snow-line (lowest level of permanent snow cover) limits agriculture.

• Atmospheric pressure and oxygen content is relatively low. This can make

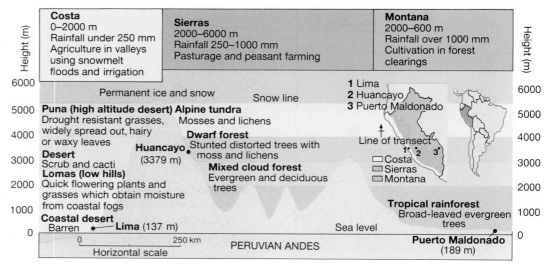

Costa	Sierras	Montana
0–2000 m	2000–6000 m	2000–600 m
Rainfall under 250 mm	Rainfall 250–1000 mm	Rainfall over 1000 m
Agriculture in valleys using snowmelt floods and irrigation	Pasturage and peasant farming	Cultivation in forest clearings

Height (m)

6000

Permanent ice and snow — Snow line

1 Lima
2 Huancayo
3 Puerto Maldonado

5000 **Puna (high altitude desert) Alpine tundra**
Drought resistant grasses, widely spread out, hairy or waxy leaves — Mosses and lichens

4000 **Dwarf forest**
Stunted distorted trees with moss and lichens

Line of transect

3000 **Desert**
Scrub and cacti — Huancayo (3379 m) — **Mixed cloud forest** Evergreen and deciduous trees

Costa
Sierras
Montana

Lomas (low hills)
2000 Quick flowering plants and grasses which obtain moisture from coastal fogs

1000 **Coastal desert**
Barren — Lima (137 m)

Tropical rainforest
Broad-leaved evergreen trees

0 — Sea level — Puerto Maldonado (189 m)

0   250 km
Horizontal scale

PERUVIAN ANDES

Height (m)
6000
5000
4000
3000
2000
1000
0

Figure C A section across the Peruvian Andes

breathing difficult, especially for new-comers to the area. Work requires more effort.

● The rarified air makes the sunlight more harmful to skin. Sunburn occurs quickly. It is easy to forget the strength of the sun because of the lower temperatures.

● A high proportion of women in these altitudes suffer from infertility. On the other hand, many Andean peoples claim to have a long life expectancy – we do not really know why this should be so.

● Soil erosion occurs easily as a result of the steep slopes, heavy rain and strong winds.

Mountain areas: other features

Mountain areas have other distinctive climatic features. Many mountain areas experience *foehn* winds. These are winds which are moist when they begin to ascend the windward sides of mountains. On rising they lose moisture through rainfall, and then descend the leeward slopes as dry winds. As they ascend they become warmer, and in winter they can bring temporary spring conditions for a few days. Foehn winds may cause avalanches by melting the snow too rapidly. They also bring trees and plants into bud very early in the year. Foehn winds occur regularly in the European Alps and in the Rockies of North America.

Transhumance is a traditional way of life in many mountain areas. It involves people making full use of the mountain environment by using the upper mountain slopes for grazing in summer. Herdsmen, or sometimes entire families, migrate to the higher slopes with their livestock in spring, returning to the valley bottoms in autumn. This happens in the Alps in Europe. The movement of communities to and from the higher pastures is closely related to the movement of the snow-line.

The train journey from Lima to Huancayo
The train to Huancayo left Lima at 7 am and climbed up to 4800 metres in 8 hours. There are 66 tunnels, 59 bridges, and 22 zigzags. Towards the highest point most of the passengers in the crowded carriage had passed out. I felt very ill.

Source unknown

We had already been travelling for three hours. The air became thinner. A doctor walked along the corridor carrying an oxygen tube. Now we were driving through wastes of snow, and at last we were on top of Galera, the highest railway station in the world (4749 metres).

I was all right, but suddenly everything turned black. I leant back in my seat, and cold sweat broke out on my forehead. I was terribly sick; my limbs ached as if I had got 'flu. The following day I felt better, but my pulse was still 120.

P. Schmidt, *Beggars on Golden Stools*

QUESTIONS

1 Which of the three places in Figure A:
   a) has the heaviest rainfall?
   b) has the highest annual temperature range?
   c) has the most even spread of temperature throughout the year?

2 a) Give *two* ways in which mountain environments are *beneficial* to human activity.
   b) Give *two* ways in which they can cause *problems* for people.

3 The railway journey from Lima to Huancayo was featured in a TV series called 'Great Railway Journeys of the World'. Read the panel and study the photographs about this journey. Make a list of the reasons why this journey was worth including in the TV series.

4 Study the section across the Peruvian Andes (Figure C).
   a) What type of vegetation might you expect to find:
      i)   on the western side at about 1500m?
      ii) on the eastern side at about 1500m?
      iii) on the eastern side at about 4500m?
   b) Explain how the climate is influencing the growth of each of your three vegetation types.
   c) Find *four* differences in the ways of life between the peoples of the Costa and Sierra.

Unit 9 ASSESSMENT

What you know

1 The world map (Figure A) locates four areas **1, 2, 3, 4**.
   a) Name each of the four areas shown.
   b) Which of the four areas:
   i)   is experiencing a lot of desertification?
   ii) has many people living in areas of high altitudes?
   iii) is dependent on monsoon rains?
   iv) is a major grain farming area?   (12 marks)

2 From the four areas **1–4**, name:
   a) *two* areas in which soil erosion is a serious problem
   b) *two* areas in tropical latitudes
   c) *two* areas in which rainfall reliability varies along a cross-section
   d) *two* areas which experience destructive storms in summer.   (8 marks)

3 For *one* area you have studied in this unit:
   a) describe how climate influences the pattern of vegetation
   b) describe how altitude influences human activities
   c) describe how climate is influenced by global pressure features.   (12 marks)

4 Explain the meaning of the following:
   Foehn wind   savanna   Humboldt current   (3 marks)

5 'One of the problems for many world peoples is the unreliability of their climate'. What evidence could you produce to justify this idea?   (5 marks)
                                          Total: 40 marks

What you understand

Study the climatic graph (Figure B):

1 Write down:
   a) the average rainfall in June
   b) the annual range of temperature
   c) the length of the rainy season.   (3 marks)

2 Is the location in the northern or southern hemisphere? Explain your answer   (3 marks)

3 Suppose the location was at a much higher altitude. How would this affect the pattern of temperature?   (3 marks)

4 To which part of the world do you think the graph might relate? Justify your choice of location.   (3 marks)
                                          Total: 12 marks

Figure A See question 1, above

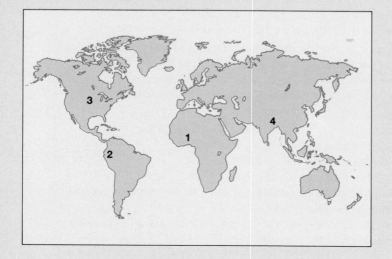

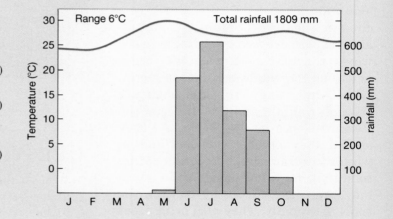

Figure B Climate graph (see exercise above)

Figure D A herder in Mali

What you can do

Study Figure C.

1 Plot the data on a graph. You will need separate vertical axes for rainfall and dust storms. **(10 marks)**

2 Describe how the pattern of rainfall:
   a) varies from year to year
   b) varies between 1960 and 1984. **(4 marks)**

3 Describe the similarities and differences between the pattern of rainfall and the pattern of dust storms. **(4 marks)**

4 Explain how the pattern of rainfall might be affecting the pattern of dust storms. **(4 marks)**

5 Suggest how the changes shown on the graph might be affecting how people live. **(4 marks)**

6 Suggest an area of the world where the changes shown on the graph might be taking place. **(2 marks)**

Total: 28 marks

Figure C Rainfall totals and dust storm frequency for a location at latitude 18′ N

Year	Rainfall (mm)	No. of days with dust storms
1965	195	—
1966	180	—
1967	120	1
1968	60	2
1969	142	4
1970	43	8
1971	20	10
1972	100	27
1973	81	42
1974	40	125
1975	190	48
1976	65	24
1977	8	28
1978	17	55
1979	35	59
1980	50	32
1981	90	42
1982	43	51
1983	8	85
1984	4	79

Details for pupil profile sheets Unit 9

Knowledge and understanding

1 Climatic features of four contrasting parts of the world

2 The relationships between climate, vegetation, and people in these four areas

3 Particular climatic features: monsoons, typhoons (hurricanes), tornadoes, foehn winds

4 Influence on climate of latitude, altitude, ocean currents

5 Influence of climatic changes on human activities

Skills

1 Interpretation of climatic data and graphs

2 Construction of climatic diagrams from data

3 Interpretation of aerial photographs showing climatic features

Values

1 Awareness of the importance of climatic uncertainty in agriculture and other human activities.

Unit 10: The green mantle

Figure shows a soil testing kit that a gardener might use. The gardener may want to test the *acidity* value of the soil or to test the levels of chemicals like nitrogen or phosphorus. Another way of testing acidity is by using a *probe meter*. This device electrical discharges in the soil move a pointer over a scale marked with acidity readings.

Figure A A soil testing kit

Soil properties

To a keen vegetable grower the acid content of the soil is of some importance. Certain vegetables can tolerate a fairly acid soil whereas others, such as cabbages or sprouts, require a soil to be alkaline, that is, low in acidity (see Figure B). Soil can often be made less acid or more alkaline by the addition of lime.

Gardeners are interested in other soil properties besides acidity. Soil *texture* and *drainage* are important. *Texture* is the balance between large and small sized particles in the soil. *Sandy* soil has mainly large particles; it drains well but plant foods are readily washed out by rainwater. *Clay* soil has mostly small particles. It keeps its plant foods

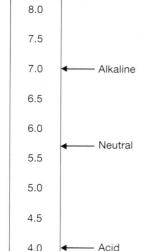

Figure B (*above*) Soil acidity guide

Figure C (*right*) The garden as an ecosystem

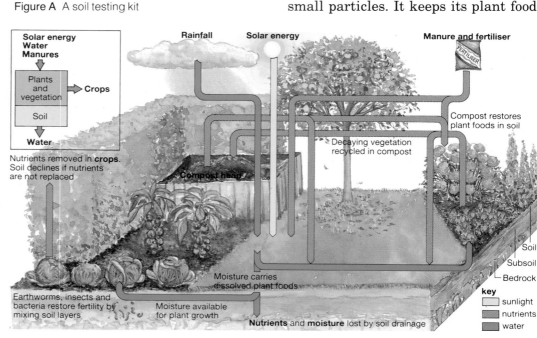

better but is sometimes badly drained and hard to dig. This is why gardeners often prefer *loamy* soils, that is, soils which have a mixture of both sand and clay in roughly equal parts. The balanced texture of loams makes them ideal for cultivation.

Soil is formed from the weathering of rock material. The parent rock gives a soil many of its characteristics. Soils formed from sandstones or gravels are likely to be sandy and acidic. Granite soils will also be acidic and probably badly drained. However soils formed from chalk or limestone rocks are likely to be alkaline and freely draining.

Other important soil properties are *drainage* and *organic content*. Organic content is the quantity of living organisms in the soil, especially micro-organisms such as bacteria. This plays a large part in determining how fertile it is.

The garden ecosystem

The good gardener understands that a garden functions as a small-scale *ecosystem* – that is, a biological system in which the different elements are in balance with each other but can change each other. Figure C shows some of the main elements in the garden ecosystem.

In a garden the gardener uses the natural pattern of the ecosystem for his own purposes, to produce vegetables or flowers. On a larger scale the farmer uses ecosystems in the same way – by becoming part of an ecosystem he can make it work to produce food.

Studying the soil

The soil is one of the most important elements of any ecosystem. The projects on this page outline some of the practical tasks you can do to study soil features further. You can do some of these exercises in someone's garden, but for others you will need to do fieldwork elsewhere. You may need to obtain the permission of the landowner concerned.

QUESTIONS

1 a) Copy this table:

Physical properties	Chemical properties	Biological properties

b) Now list under the correct headings the following soil properties:

acidity	organic content	nitrogen content
texture	phosphorus content	drainage

2 Write down:
  a) an advantage of a sandy soil
  b) an advantage of a clay soil

3 A market gardener is considering setting up his business in an area of sandy soil. Advise him of the soil problems he might encounter and the measures he should take.

4 'The fertility of the soil mostly depends on how people use it.' Do you think this is true? Give reasons for your answer.

Fieldwork

5 a) Using a soil testing kit or probe meter, compare the soil acidity in two gardens some distance away from each other. Record the results under headings:

site location	soil texture
rock type	degree of cultivation
acidity reading (pH value)	

Try to explain any differences you find.

  b) Repeat the exercise on different types of land cover – for instance, pasture, heath, pine woodland, deciduous woodland. Does soil acidity seem to be related to land cover?

6 Use your soil samples from question 5 to do a simple test to determine soil texture. First take a handful of soil and wet it slightly. Then rub it between your fingers, feeling for the grainy particles. Look at the table below to classify your sample.

Soil classification

Soil texture	What the soil feels like when wet
sand	feels gritty; not sticky even when wet
sandy loam	can be rolled into a thread with difficulty; not sticky
loam	rolls easily into a thread; not sticky
clay loam	sticky; easily forms a thread
clay	very sticky; easily moulded into any shape

  a) Is there much variation in the texture of the samples?
  b) Which samples will be the easiest for cultivation?
  c) Which will be the most difficult?

10.2 Woodland study

Some pupils carried out two soil and vegetation surveys of a wooded area at Hawley in north-eastern Hampshire. Their results are shown in Figure A. Look at the *soil profile* of Location 1. A soil profile is a cross-section through the soil to show its different layers. This profile was made by digging a pit down to the rock beneath. Easier ways of making a soil profile include:

- using a soil augur to screw into the soil and lift the different layers to the surface
- looking out for a place where the soil is already exposed, for example along a cutting in the roadside.

The soil at Location 1 is a type called a *podsol*. The layers can be identified by their colour. The upper layers are dark brown, almost black. These contain a lot of humus, or plant food, from the decay of the trees above. Beneath is a much paler, greyish layer. The pale colour is caused by *leaching*; rainwater seeps down through the soil and washes out the plant foods which give the soil its dark colour. Lower down in the profile the soil is dark again. Here the soil minerals washed downwards have collected into a hard layer or 'pan'. This layer can sometimes become so hard that it stops the water from draining through and causes waterlogging at the surface.

Soil and vegetation

The pupils found that there were several different sorts of trees and shrubs including birch, hazel, holly, rhododendron, and sweet chestnut in the wood. But most of the trees were *coniferous* types such as pine or spruce. These grow well on the podsolic soil because they can tolerate the podsol's high acidity.

Using measuring tapes the pupils took a 30 metre long *transect* of the wood at a sample point at Location 1. At every metre they noted the species of tree closest to the metre mark, taking care not to count the same tree twice. They then made some more transects chosen at random across the same site, and averaged out the results. Using tree identification books they drew up a table of how often each tree species occurred.

Figure A Pupil's results for vegetation surveys

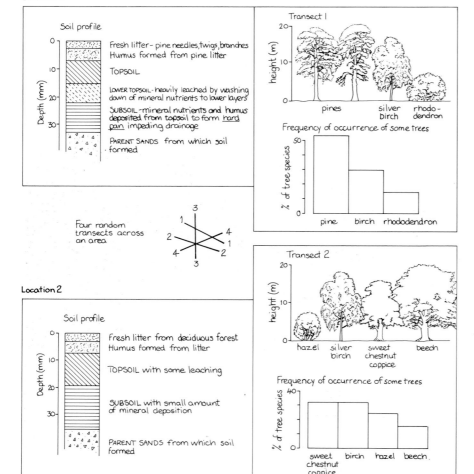

Figure B Woodland layers

They used these results to draw the *histogram* shown next to the soil profile. A histogram is a sort of bar chart which shows how some categories of things occur more often than others.

Before doing the field work the pupils had studied the diagram shown in Figure B. This diagram shows the different layers that might be expected to occur in a typical woodland. They were asked to note which layers seemed to be most important in their sample wood. The pupils found that the tree layer was especially well developed. The canopies of the pines grew so close to each other that little light penetrated further down. This meant that shrubs had little chance to grow. Where the wood opened out, however, rhododendron and other shrubs were growing well, often up to 10 metres high. The field and ground layers were mostly poor because of the shade from the trees. Instead the ground was covered by a layer of 'litter' of pine cones and needles, several inches thick.

The exercises were repeated at other sample locations within the woods. In this way they were able to compare the variations they found in soil and vegetation type. Their results for another site (Location 2) are also shown in Figure A.

Vegetation change

The wood at Hawley is not a 'natural' vegetation. There is almost no natural vegetation left anywhere in the British Isles. Over the centuries man has continued to modify the vegetation for his own needs. Our vegetation is therefore almost always 'man-made'.

At one time the vegetation at Hawley was oak forest, a *deciduous* wood. Prehistoric man's grazing animals ate the young shoots and prevented the wood from continuing to grow. As a result much of the area turned into a heathland of rough grass and bracken. It stayed like this until the nineteenth century when the area was turned into a country estate. The new landowner planted the pinewoods and rhododendron to help in the breeding of game for shooting. Pine trees produce an acid litter and the soil has gradually become more podsolic in character.

Modern man is also changing the Hawley ecosystem. The area is now owned by the army, which uses it for training. The vehicles churn up the ground so that the soil is washed away by the rain. Without care some parts of the wood may soon not be able to support trees at all.

Figure C Hawley Woods

QUESTIONS

1 Describe or explain what is meant by:
   a) leaching
   b) a histogram

2 Name *three* characteristics of a podsol.

3 What equipment do you need to produce a soil profile? How would you use it?

4 Study the pupils' results for Location 2 (Figure A):
   a) Give *two* ways in which the soil and vegetation of Location 2 is *similar* to Location 1.
   b) Give *three* ways in which the soil and vegetation of the two locations differ and give a reason for the differences.

5 Why do you think there is hardly any natural vegetation left in Britain? In what sorts of places would you be most likely to find it? Why?

6 'In an ecosystem soil and vegetation are always closely related.' What evidence of this have you found in this study?

10.3 Wetlands under threat

The Norfolk Broads is a region of marshes, creeks, and shallow ponds in East Anglia, mostly in the area west of Great Yarmouth (Figure A). The Broads were formed in the Middle Ages when people cut peat for fuel in the marshy areas. The peat diggings lay below the water table and gradually flooded. Eventually they became linked to the rivers, forming a continuous system of waterways. Areas where much of the ground lies under water, like the Broads, are called *wetlands*.

The Broads support a varied ecosystem of bird, plant, and insect life. The shallow waters are colonized by plants such as reed, bulrush, and sedge. The banks often have a growth of trees like the alder or willow, which grow well in damp areas. Many flowering plants that are rare in Britain as a whole are common in the Broads.

The banks and reeds form habitats or homes for water birds such as mallard, coot, and heron. Many birds nest in the Broads from season to season. For instance the black tern is an early summer visitor. Birds of prey, such as the marsh harrier and kestrel, prey on small water mammals, particularly the water vole and water shrew. A distinc-

Figure A The Norfolk Broads, showing the location of Cockshoot Broad

Figure B Problems in the Norfolk Broads and their solution

The problem area	What's gone wrong?	What can be done?
Water quality Cloudy, muddy water with no plant or insect life	Water has become polluted, encouraging the growth of algae (microscopic water plants). Dead algae form an oozy mud which is filling up the Broads and preventing natural weed growth. Motor boat propellors stimulate algal growth by churning up the water.	Isolate and mud-pump, as at Cockshoot Broad. Only possible with private Broads.
Bank erosion Banks wearing away up to 3 metres in 10 years	Poor water quality reduces reed and sedge growth at the banks. Banks now less protected from wash of increasing numbers of pleasure boats. Fewer wildfowl and nesting birds because of fewer habitats.	Design a new type of boat hull that makes less wash; long and thin, instead of short and squat.
Changing marshland Loss of wildlife habitats in the marshes	Reeds and sedges no longer cropped for thatch and marsh hay. More marshland being shaded out by tree growth, which is taking over many marshes.	Regular management of the marshes to limit excessive tree growth and give marshland species a proper chance to develop.
Grazing marshes A quarter of grazing marshes have been lost to farmland by draining	Cereal farming more profitable than cattle. Farmers given grants to drain and convert marshland to crops.	Pay farmers grants to make it more profitable for them to graze rather than crop the marshes.

tive insect of the Broads is the swallow-tail butterfly, which needs the milk parsley plant as food for its larvae.

People and the Broads

People have always lived in the Broads and used the ecosystem for their own purposes. Reeds and sedges were harvested regularly for thatching and for 'marsh hay' for cattle. Large areas of damp marshland were used as grazing marshes for the cattle of local farmers. Some people lived on the banks by the rivers, and made a living by trapping eels which were sold for food. People were a part of the ecosystem, using it but not disrupting it.

During the last century people have become much more of a threat to the Broadland ecosystem, almost destroying it. We no longer seem to recognize how delicate the ecosystem is. The table (Figure B) shows how we are misusing the area. Recently people have become concerned about the damage to the Broads. What do you think can be done to overcome the problems?

Cockshoot Broad

Find Cockshoot Broad on the map (Figure A). This was once noted for the abundance of its waterfowl, but in recent years hardly any birds visited the area. This was because no plant life could grow in the muddy, polluted water. The pollution here, and elsewhere in the Broads, was caused by concentrations of phosphate and nitrogen levels in the surface layers of the mud at the bottom of the water. This highly enriched mud allowed algae to breed, which in turn made it impossible for water plants to live. In most respects it was a 'dead' Broad.

Cockshoot Broad (see photograph, Figure C) was used for an experiment to see how dead Broads could be restored. A mud pump was used to suction-dredge the surface mud from the bottom

of the Broad. At the same time dams were built to cut off water from polluting rivers. In three months, 40 000 cubic metres of mud was dredged – enough to fill forty-four olympic-sized swimming pools.

Within a month of the start of the scheme, the water was clear enough to see the bottom. Within two or three months, seeds which had been buried by dredged mud for thirty years began to germinate. Waterlilies and waterweeds began to grow, although many of the young plants were eaten by birds eager to return to Cockshoot Broad. Scientific tests showed that phosphate and nitrogen levels in the water had fallen considerably.

A temporary ecosystem

The Norfolk Broads are really a temporary or transitional ecosystem. Left alone without human interference, the Broads would gradually dry out in the same way that Fleet Pond (page 7) is drying out.

People want to stop this happening and to preserve the Broads as they are for our use and pleasure. To be successful in this, we must learn to *manage* the Broads ecosystem. This means understanding how it works, and how it can be damaged beyond repair by careless overuse.

Figure C Cockshoot Broad

QUESTIONS

1 Name some examples of plant, animal, and bird life which make the Broads a distinctive ecosystem.

2 Describe *four* ways in which the Broads ecosystem has been damaged by man in recent years.

3 Give some reasons why the restoration of Cockshoot Broad was so successful. Why might it be difficult to restore the rivers and other Broads in the same way?

4 Assume that the Broads Authority has decided to ban all power boating on the Broads and rivers within its area in order to conserve wildlife and restore water quality. Write a newspaper article outlining the effects of this on people's activities. In your article suggest other ways in which the Authority could solve the problem.

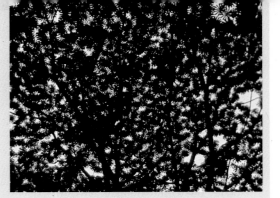

Step into virgin rainforest and you enter stillness. It is hard to see anything of the teeming wildlife. It is a strange twilight, almost windless world. Great tree trunks soar high above, rising 70 ft or more before they sprout branches. It is a bit like being in a giant wooden cathedral; if you tip your head right back and look straight up the columns of the trees you can just see its intricate green roof.

Figure A (*below*) Tropical rainforest in the Amazon Basin, South America

Rainforest is the most widely occurring of the world's natural forests (see panel). It covers an area of 3.5 million square miles, about the size of the United States. About three-fifths of it is in Central and South America. Most of the rest is in West Africa and South-East Asia. Another name for tropical rainforest is *selva*.

Figure B (*above*) Climate data for Manaus, Brazil

The forest as an ecosystem

The climatic graph (Figure B) for Manaus, in the Amazon Basin of Brazil, shows the type of climate needed for the growth of tropical rainforest. Manaus lies close to the Equator, so that the sun is overhead and temperatures are high throughout the year. There is about three or four times as much rain per year as in Britain, and there is no dry season. In areas like this it usually rains heavily every day. Without any seasons the forest is continually growing, dying, and being renewed.

The high temperatures mean that fungi and soil micro-organisms like bacteria can breed very quickly. They feed on the remains of dying trees and plants, so that decaying vegetation is very quickly broken down by soil organisms into new plant foods. The abundant moisture means that plant foods are rapidly carried in solution to the growing trees and plants. For this reason the soils of selvas have very little litter (plant debris) or humus (new plant food). This makes it very different from the soils you have studied in the previous sections.

Tropical forest soils support a huge *biomass*. This is the total amount of organic growth (trees, plants, animals, soil organisms) in an ecosystem. Be-

Figure C (*below*) Forest layers and processes at work in the forest (see question 4)

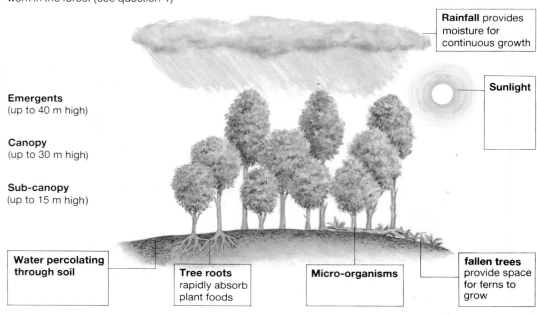

Rainfall provides moisture for continuous growth

Sunlight

Emergents
(up to 40 m high)

Canopy
(up to 30 m high)

Sub-canopy
(up to 15 m high)

Water percolating through soil

Tree roots rapidly absorb plant foods

Micro-organisms

fallen trees provide space for ferns to grow

cause of this it is easy to think that the forest soils must be very fertile, but this is not true. The ecosystem is supported not because of the soil fertility but because plant foods are recycled through the system so quickly. Tropical forest soils are not very fertile. They are heavily leached by the rainfall and contain few plant nutrients.

Tropical forest and man

The selva ecosystem is very complex, with plants, trees, and animals all dependent on each other for survival. It is also a very fragile ecosystem which functions well as long as man does not interfere with it too much.

Humankind is highly dependent on the tropical rainforest. Besides providing a way of life for the few remaining native Indians, the forest provides a huge range of resources for the world at large. It is said that each time we read a book, drive a car, drink coffee, or take a pill we are likely to be using something from the rainforest. Figure D shows the many things which come from the forest. Even the air we breathe may have been 'manufactured' by the forest. The plants convert atmospheric carbon dioxide into oxygen.

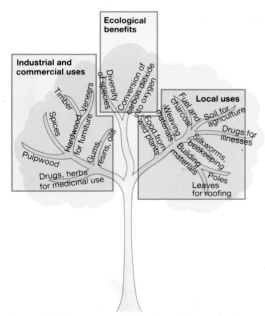

Figure D The uses and benefits of the tropical rainforest to people

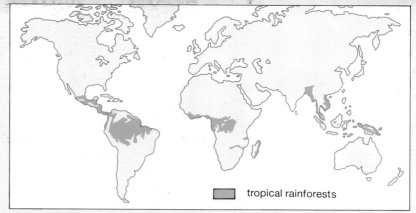

tropical rainforests

Features of tropical forest

● Tropical rainforest grows to a great height. The tallest trees, or *emergents*, reach over 40 metres high. Below is a *canopy* formed by the crowns of other large trees. Even the smaller trees beneath the canopy can reach 15 metres above the ground (see Figure C).

● Very little sunlight breaks through the canopy, so there is often little ground growth. You can walk without difficulty along the forest floor because it is so open, but it is easy to get lost since it all looks the same. Where the canopy is broken a dense layer of ferns and lianas (creepers) develops.

● Most tropical rainforest is *evergreen*. This means that there is no season of the year when all the trees shed their leaves.

Instead individual trees lose their leaves at different times. The forest has a continuous green appearance all the year round.

● There are many different species. Ten square kilometres of selva may contain 750 species of tree and 1500 flowering plant species. In the same area there may also be up to 400 types of birds, 150 kinds of butterfly, 100 different types of reptiles and 60 species of amphibian. Much of this wildlife lives in the forest canopy.

● In low, wet areas along flood plains and deltas *peaty swamp forest* is found. This has slim, short trees rising above the swamp. In mountain rain shadow areas the evergreen forest gives way to *tropical moist deciduous forest* because of the variable rainfall.

QUESTIONS

1 Look around your home or classroom. Make a list of the things which may have come from tropical rainforests. (Figure D) will help you.

2 Use your atlases to list the countries which contain parts of the Amazon rainforest.

3 Describe the features of the different layers of the tropical rainforest.

4 Figure C shows some of the processes at work within the rainforest. Copy the diagram and complete the labels.

5 Explain the role of the following in the tropical rainforest ecosystem:
   a) sunlight and high temperatures
   b) rainfall and moisture
   c) soil organisms

10.5 Tropical forests 2: gone tomorrow

Once it used to take a team of men a whole day to hack down a giant tree with axes. Then, with the arrival of the chain-saw, a single man could do the job in about ten minutes. Now machines can chew an entire tree, branches and all, into small chips in sixty seconds flat.

Some South American Indians have a legend which says that the trees hold up the sky. They believe that if the trees are cut down there will be a catastrophe.

Figure A Satellite photograph of rainforest clearance

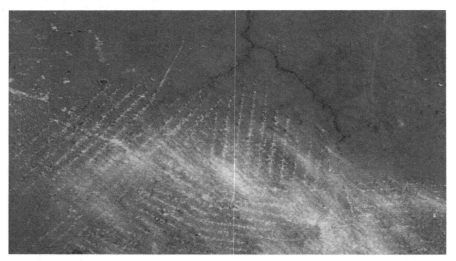

The map of tropical forests on the previous page shows rainforest *lands*, not all of which still support forest. The areas of true rainforest are now retreating as more and more forest is cleared. Figures A and B show how and where *deforestation* is taking place.

Until modern times tropical forests all over the world used to support native populations. People used to 'farm' the forests by 'slash-and-burn' agriculture. With this type of farming the forest soil was used to provide crops

Figure B (*below*) Areas where deforestation is taking place (see question 3)

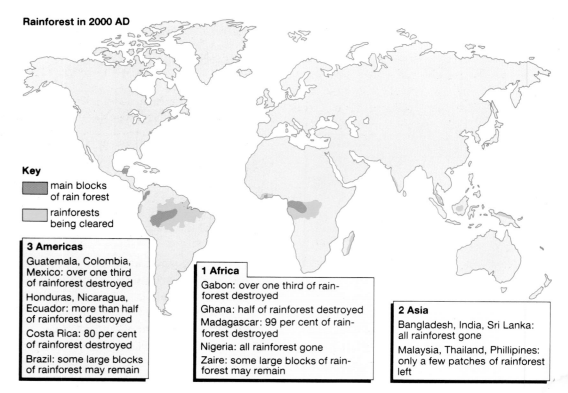

Rainforest in 2000 AD

Key
- main blocks of rain forest
- rainforests being cleared

3 Americas
Guatemala, Colombia, Mexico: over one third of rainforest destroyed
Honduras, Nicaragua, Ecuador: more than half of rainforest destroyed
Costa Rica: 80 per cent of rainforest destroyed
Brazil: some large blocks of rainforest may remain

1 Africa
Gabon: over one third of rainforest destroyed
Ghana: half of rainforest destroyed
Madagascar: 99 per cent of rainforest destroyed
Nigeria: all rainforest gone
Zaire: some large blocks of rainforest may remain

2 Asia
Bangladesh, India, Sri Lanka: all rainforest gone
Malaysia, Thailand, Phillipines: only a few patches of rainforest left

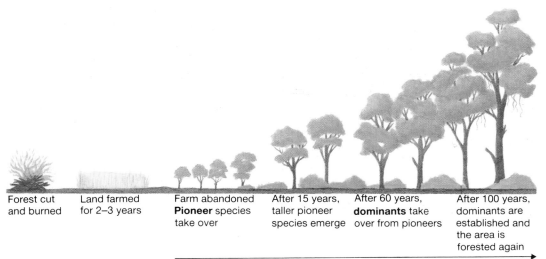

Forest cut and burned | Land farmed for 2–3 years | Farm abandoned **Pioneer** species take over | After 15 years, taller pioneer species emerge | After 60 years, **dominants** take over from pioneers | After 100 years, dominants are established and the area is forested again

Plant succession

Figure C Forest clearance and recovery

Figure D 'Slash and burn' clearance in Nigeria

in small clearings, but the forest as an ecosystem was not damaged (Figure C).

In the last forty years about half the world's rainforest has been felled. The increased demand for hardwoods, especially from the United States and Japan has led to the clearance of huge areas of forest. A Japanese company is said to be transforming an entire rainforest in Papua New Guinea into packaging for calculators. In South and Central America forests have been felled to provide land for new cattle ranches and settlements for homeless peasants. Over 20 million hectares of tropical forest are being cleared every year.

The clearances affect not just the forest itself but also the soil, rivers, the atmosphere, and people throughout the world (Figure B).

Conserving the forest

Some tropical countries are now realizing the need to conserve and properly manage their forest resources. The Korup area (Figure D) of Cameroon in Africa is being set aside as a national park. It is intended to move the Korup people to new areas on the fringes of the park where they have the same sort of environment but better land and soil.

How do you think they will feel about this? Apart from limited tourism, the rest of the Korup forest will be left alone for scientists to study its character and potential.

QUESTIONS

1 Give *two* reasons why so much tropical forest clearance is taking place.

2 Figure A shows an area of rainforest which is undergoing clearance.
  a) From the colour key distinguish the cleared areas from those Wstill forested.
  b) Cover the image with a piece of tracing paper. Trace off and Wcolour in the deforested areas. Convert your tracing paper into a map showing the extent of deforestation.
  c) Try to find features on the image which might tell you more about how the deforestation has occurred. Are the cleared areas close to roads or tracks? How are they now being used?

3 **a)** Make an outline copy of the world map in Figure B.
  b) Copy the information in boxes **1**, **2** and **3** and draw lines from Wthe boxes to the correct locations on the map.
  c) Give your map a title.

4 Explain the different ways in which tropical deforestation might affect:
  a) native peoples of the forest
  b) people living downstream from the forest, who depend on rice growing and fishing
  c) a manufacturer in Europe or North America
  d) people living in coastal cities

5 'There is no need to conserve the tropical forest because there is so much of it.' What do you think of this viewpoint?

Soil is a resource we often take for granted. Figure A shows some of the ways in which soil is put at risk. Although actual erosion is carried out by the rain and wind, it is often our careless management of the soil which begins the process of erosion.

Soil erosion is a major problem for humankind. Each year, 75 billion tonnes of soil are washed from the surface of the land. This results in the loss of 11 million hectares of arable land. At this rate, by the end of the century, 18 per cent of the world's arable land could have disappeared. By 2025 the same amount again could go. It takes much longer for soil to form than it does to destroy it. The formation of 2.5 cm depth of topsoil from a bare rock surface can take anything from 100 to 2500 years, depending on the soil type. This same depth of soil can be destroyed in as little as ten years.

Where is soil erosion happening?

Soil erosion is occurring in every continent (see Figure B). One of the worst erosion 'hotspots' is the USA. A third of American croplands are losing their long-term productivity because of soil erosion. Many areas have lost more than 75 per cent of their topsoil in recent years. Although overuse of these areas brought about the 'Dust Bowl' in the USA in the 1930s (page 96), economic factors still encourage farmers to try to achieve record harvests.

Soil erosion in North America is serious for people everywhere. The USA is the world's biggest exporter of grain. If American grain production here fell, it would cause hunger problems for many Third World countries.

Deforestation is a major cause of soil erosion. Removal of forest for agriculture in the foothills of the Himalayas in Nepal, India, and Bangladesh has brought about serious erosion of the steep hillslopes. The erosion has greatly increased the silt loads of the rivers Ganges and Brahmaputra, causing the river channels to become blocked. In-

What causes soil erosion?
Natural processes Soil naturally moves downslope under its own gravity by soil creep. Even on steep slopes creep takes place very slowly provided that the slope is covered with vegetation.

Human activities greatly increase the rate of soil loss from slopes:

Deforestation produces bare hillslopes which are only slowly recolonised by forest.

Overgrazing is the nibbling away of pasture by grazing animals quicker than it can grow again. This produces bare patches of ground easily eroded by the wind or rain.

Overproduction from agricultural land exhausts the soil of nutrients and humus so that it crumbles into dust.

Modern farming requires large fields with few hedgerows or tree cover. Bare soil is left unprotected from the wind.

Cultivation loosens the natural soil structure. Bare surfaces left uncropped are soon made into gullies by rainfall.

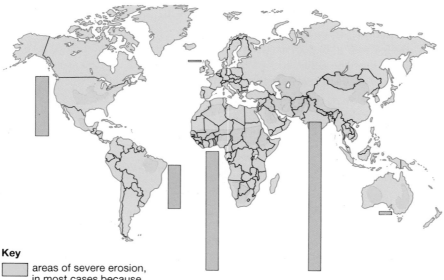

Key

areas of severe erosion, in most cases because of overgrazing, overcultivation and mismanagement

Annual loss of soil : 75 billion tonnes
The height of the blocks is proportional to the amount of soil lost from the land surface

Figure A (*top left*) Causes of soil erosion

Figure B (*left*) Soil erosion worldwide

creased flooding along the plains of these rivers, has put at risk the homes and livelihoods of 500 million people.

The silt from the erosion ends up in the Bay of Bengal. It is building up a huge shallow area of 5 million hectares off the shore of the continent. One day it will break the surface of the sea and become an island. Some people think it will cause a political dispute between India and Bangladesh over which country it belongs to. Others think it should be given to Nepal, since the earth for it originally came from Nepal. What do you think?

What can be done?

Soil erosion can only be halted by the *management* of the soil rather than just the *use* of it. Some of the main techniques of soil management or conservation are:

● *Terracing* Building up cultivated hillsides into terraces prevents bare soil from being washed downhill by rainwater. Rice paddy fields in the Philippines have been terraced for over 2000 years (Figure D).

● *Hardy animals* Native drought-resistant breeds of cattle, goats, and sheep are better for lands with dry soil than the scientifically bred varieties of western countries. They may not produce as much meat or milk but can live on less forage.

● *Rotation* of crops so that the ground is not continually exhausted of the same group of nutrients.

● *Interplanting* of different crops so that the ground is never left entirely bare when a crop is lifted.

● *Organic farming* using farm wastes such as manure to replace lost nutrients. These maintain the soil structure more effectively than chemicals.

● *Windbreaks* of trees reduce the impact of wind erosion.

● *Selective tree planting* Some trees are able to survive drought conditions and poor soil. They provide fodder for ani-

mals and their roots stabilize the soil and supply nutrients to it.

● *Rotational grazing* gives over-grazed pastures time to recover. Bare pasture can also be improved by planting legume grasses such as clover and livestock. These help to restore soil fertility.

Figure C (*above left*) The Guangzhou (Pearl) River is coloured yellow by the soil load it carries into the South China Sea

Figure D (*above*) Terraced rice paddies in Indonesia

QUESTIONS

1 Produce a summary of the world soil erosion map by making a table with two columns. Use these column headings:
    Continent   Regions of the continent
Use the information in Figure B to complete your table.

2 Explain why soil erosion is such a big problem:
  a) to the grain farmers of the USA
  b) to the peasant farmers of the Ganges valley
  c) to you or me

3 Which methods of soil conservation would be of most use to:
  a) a rice farmer in a hilly area?
  b) a cereal grower in Norfolk?
  c) a pastoralist in north Africa?

4 Study an atlas map of the United States. From Figure B find the area in the USA which is experiencing most soil erosion.
  a) What is the cause of soil erosion in this part of the United States?
  b) What could be the consequences for American farmers?
  c) What could be the consequences for other countries?
  d) When did this area experience soil erosion previously?
  e) What do you think happens to the soil which is eroded in the American grain lands? Where does it all go?
  f) Where do you think the soil from the American grain lands is finally being deposited?

5 'Soil erosion is a major problem for mankind.' Do you think it is a bigger problem than some of the other problems in this book? Why?

Unit 10 ASSESSMENT

What you know

1 Name and describe *three* inputs into a soil system.
(6 marks)

2 Name and describe *three* causes of soil erosion.
(6 marks)

3 What pH value might you expect to obtain from
a) an acid soil?
b) an alkaline soil
(2 marks)

4 Which areas of the world contain most of the world's tropical forests?
(2 marks)

5 Give examples of the sorts of bird and plant life that make the Norfolk Broads distinctive.
(3 marks)

6 Describe *three* ways in which you could record a soil profile. What are the uses of soil profiles?
(5 marks)

7 What is meant by the following:
soil acidity   organic content of soil
leaching   soil texture
(4 marks)

8 a) What *four* layers might you expect to find in a mature vegetation community?
b) Why are some layers more developed than others? Give examples.
(7 marks)

9 Find *four* ways in which the structure and composition of a tropical rainforest differs from that of a woodland in Hampshire.
(8 marks)

10 What is meant by *plant succession*? Give examples.
(4 marks)

11 Discuss the ways in which tropical deforestation is affecting:
a) local people in a rainforest area
b) people the world over
(4 marks)

12 For any *two* of the ecosystems you have studied in this book, compare how:
a) people once made use of the system without damaging it
b) people now damage or disrupt the system   (4 marks)

13 'People are now showing more concern for natural ecosystems.' Does this seem to be true from the ecosystems you have studied in this book?   (5 marks)
Total: 60 marks

Figure A Sketch map of activities in a forested area

What you understand

Study the map (Figure A) and photograph (Figure B).

1 Identify the type of ecosystem which the illustrations show.
(1 mark)

2 What layers in the vegetation structure would you expect to be most developed?
(4 marks)

3 What type of soil would you expect to find with this vegetation? Describe some of its features.
(3 marks)

4 The area indicated on the map is experiencing marked soil erosion.
a) What might be causing the erosion?
b) What could be done about it?
(6 marks)

5 a) In what ways are people using the ecosystem?
b) How are these uses likely to be damaging it?
c) Suggest what might be done to limit this damage.
(6 marks)
Total: 20 marks

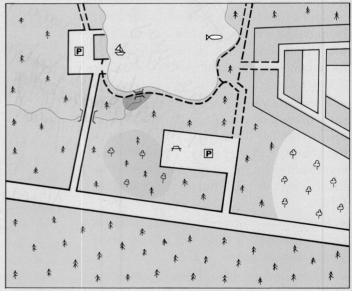

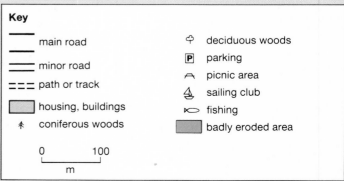

Key

—— main road	⚘ deciduous woods
—— minor road	P parking
=== path or track	⌐ picnic area
▨ housing, buildings	⚓ sailing club
✦ coniferous woods	⤢ fishing
	▨ badly eroded area

0   100
m

What you can do

Assume that you wish to investigate more fully the ecosystem shown in Figures A and B.

a) Draw up a list of the equipment and other materials you might need to organize a field study for a class of twenty. (5 marks)

b) Produce a list of the tasks which the class will need to carry out. (5 marks)

c) For any *one* task write a detailed explanation of how to carry it out. (5 marks)

d) Compare your lists and outline with those of friends. Who has produced the clearest guidelines for the field study? (5 marks)

Total: 20 marks

Figure B An area of coniferous forest in Alberta, Canada

Details for pupil profile sheets Unit 10

Knowledge and understanding

1 Concept of ecosystems and their elements: inputs, outputs, biomass

2 Factors that influence how ecosystems develop – people, climate, etc.

3 Knowledge of soil properties – acidity, texture, drainage, organic content

4 Knowledge of structure of vegetation communities – layering, composition

5 Features, structure, functioning, distribution of specific ecosystems: domestic garden, coniferous woodland, wetland, tropical rain forest

6 How ecosystems are at risk from nature and from man, e.g. deforestation, soil erosion

Skills

1 Use of equipment to measure soil acidity and texture

2 Use of equipment to measure structure of vegetation community and presentation of results

3 Making and evaluating decisions about use of ecosystems

4 Assessment of vegetation change from satellite image

Values

1 Awareness of ways in which people
   a) can use and become part of ecosystems
   b) can overuse, damage and destroy ecosystems
   c) can remedy the problems of b)

2 Awareness of feelings which people may have for particular ecosystems

Unit 11: Planet care

Los Angeles is one of the world's largest cities and also one of the wealthiest. Some ten million people live in or around Los Angeles. Many of them earn high salaries, live in expensive homes, and enjoy a high quality of life. To many Americans, Los Angeles is a very desirable city in which to live. Many rich people from the business and entertainment worlds have made their homes in the suburbs of Beverley Hills and Hollywood.

But Los Angeles is also one of the world's most disaster-prone cities. Out of 13 major natural hazards, Los Angeles suffers from no fewer than eight. Look at Figure A to see which they are. The worst problems for Los Angeles are these:

Figure A Hazards in and around Los Angeles

Earthquakes The Los Angeles area is criss-crossed by a pattern of 'active' faults, including the San Andreas Fault (page 17). In 1971 the San Fernando Valley earthquake damaged 1000 buildings and several motorways. If a nearby dam had burst 80000 people could have been drowned. Scientists think that another huge earthquake soon is inevitable. It could cause devastation for up to 65 km from its centre. Nevertheless they also think that they could predict it early enough to evacuate high-rise buildings and turn off all mains services. An earthquake did occur in 1987, but its damage was localized.

Tsunamis A major earthquake could produce a tidal wave or tsunami which would devastate the beach and coastal areas around the city where many new suburbs have developed in recent years.

Sinking coasts Oil extraction in the Long Beach area has been causing the coastline to sink. To stop the subsi-

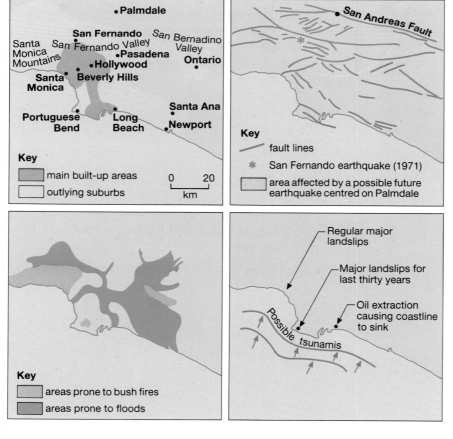

Figure B A landslip closing part of the Pacific Highway

Figure C Fire in the chaparral vegetation

Figure D Smog over Los Angeles

Figure E Some people's ideas about living in Los Angeles

1 'In and around Los Angeles man has meddled with his environment – he has polluted the air, the sea, and the scenery'

2 'Ten million Angelenos are powerless in the face of natural hazards over which they have no control'

3 'Few people think that taking out earthquake insurance is worthwhile'

4 'Periods of time between floods are sometimes long, whereas the memories of people are short'

5 'If a photochemical smog had come down on the first settlers of Los Angeles they would have immediately fled into the hills'

6 'To many people Los Angeles remains a city of challenge and opportunity – where man has tamed his environment on the way to achieving the world's most advanced urban society'

dence, water had to be injected into the beds from which the oil had been pumped. Fortunately no tsunami occurred while the coast was still sinking.

Landslides Slopes in the Los Angeles area are very unstable, especially in wet, winter weather. Along the coast, landslides occur where loose sands and gravels overlie clays. Other slopes have been over-steepened to make way for new roads. The Pacific Coast Highway is sometimes closed by landslides (Figure B).

Winds The 'Santa Ana' is a hot, dry wind which frequently causes brush fires in the surrounding countryside in the summer (Figure C). In recent years many suburbs have expanded into these brushwood areas.

Floods Streams and rivers are prone to heavy discharges and floods for several reasons. These include:

● mountainous or hilly landscape with steep gradients

● brushwood fires causing soil erosion and increased runoff

● widespread street paving, roads, roofs increasing runoff.

Streams therefore have flash responses. Powerful discharges can move boulders up to 20 tonnes in weight. Half the built-up area of Los Angeles is flood-prone, with three million inhabitants at risk.

Drought Los Angeles makes huge demands on surrounding water resources for industry, drinking, home, and leisure. The surrounding area includes much desert with water shortages. The city has to 'import' most of its water from the Owens Valley and the Colorado River (page 52). Many people now think that there are no more water resources which Los Angeles can use.

Smog A survey showed that half the population can expect to experience eye irritation from photochemical smog for about a third of the days in any year. This makes Los Angeles much worse for atmospheric pollution than any other American city (Figure D). The smog is caused mainly by fumes from car exhausts. These are converted by sunlight into ozone. Traffic queues also cause large concentrations of carbon monoxide. Ozone levels are monitored and warnings issued by radio and television when concentrations become dangerous to health. Sea breezes help to keep the smog away from many parts of the city.

QUESTIONS

1 Which natural hazards occur most frequently in Los Angeles?

2 For each of the locations 1, 2 and 3 on the map:
   a) identify the natural hazards which it has recently experienced or might experience
   b) state in which of the three places you would prefer to live.

3 Look at the 'frequency of occurrence' table.
   a) Draw up a comparable list for your own home area
   b) Is Los Angeles a more hazardous place than where you live?
   c) Is the frequency of occurrence of hazards much different?

4 Look at the 'views' of Los Angeles (Figure E). Choose one of these views as a topic for an essay or discussion. Write about the ideas that seem to be behind the viewpoint. Do you think the viewpoint is justified?

11.2 World environmental problems

In trying to change the environment for their own purposes, people have created new environmental problems. Some of these problems are now so large that they threaten the existence of life itself in many parts of the world. Here is a summary of the most important ones.

Deforestation

In 1950, 15 per cent of the earth's land surface was covered by tropical forest. By 1985 this had declined to 10 per cent, and by 2000 no more than 7 per cent of the land may be covered (see pages 112–115). Tropical forests contain a huge stock of resources which mankind has only just begun to learn about, and these may now be lost forever.

Tropical forests help to control the amount of carbon dioxide in the atmosphere. The loss of forests is causing carbon dioxide levels to increase. This in turn is causing *global warming*.

Desertification

Over a third of the earth's ice-free land area is desert or is being desertified. Each year some 12 million hectares become agriculturally worthless. Eighty million people living in these

Figure C Dust storm in the Sahel.

areas are now at risk. The world map shows where most desertification is taking place (see also pages 28 and 98).

Soil erosion

Soil erosion can be a product of deforestation or desertification (see page 116). It also results from over-farming. Soil erosion is occurring in many underdeveloped countries where population pressure means the land is worked to exhaustion. It is also occurring more and more in developed countries because farmers are replacing lost nutrients not with organic substances like manure but with chemicals. These produce high yields but contribute nothing to the well-being of the soil.

Genetic erosion

At one time there were very many different varieties of cereals like maize or rice. Although each was vulnerable to certain pests and diseases, not all varieties of the cereal were liable to attack by the same ones. Scientists have concentrated only on breeding plants with high yielding strains of cereals and have discarded the rest. This has increased the chances of destruction of the world cereal crop by a single pest or disease. Some scientists have now set up 'seed banks' in which samples of the older traditional varieties of cereals are stored.

Extinction of plant and animal

Figure A Forest clearance in the Amazon rainforest

Figure B Desertification on a world scale

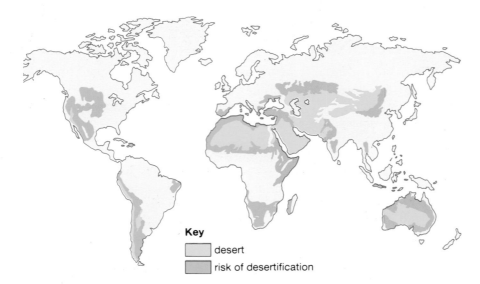

Key
- desert
- risk of desertification

Acid rain

This is the effect of acids dissolved in rain on forests, rivers, and lakes (Figure D). The worst affected areas are Sweden, Norway, parts of central Europe, and eastern North America. Some 18 000 lakes in Sweden alone are now so acidified that they have hardly any fish.

Tracing the cause of acid rain is like a 'whodunit' detective story – there are many clues but no proof of the culprit. Many people now believe it to be industrial pollution, especially from coal and oil-fired power stations (Figure D). Norway and Sweden claim that most of their acid rain comes from Britain. The United Nations has started an environmental programme to try to solve the problem.

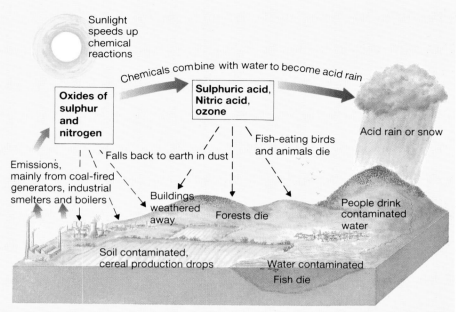

Figure D Effects of acid rain

The ozone crisis

This is caused by gases called chlorofluorocarbons (CFCs) escaping into the atmosphere. CFCs are released by aerosol sprays, air-cooling systems in refrigerators and also in the manufacture of some foam packaging. They escape into the upper atmosphere where they attack the ozone layer. This layer protects life from the sun's ultraviolet rays.

Figure E shows the effects of this. Many scientists suggest that the destruction of the ozone layer is the most serious crisis the world now faces.

Scientists think that the increased amounts of CFCs and carbon dioxide in the atmosphere will retain heat from the earth's surface. The result may be a 'greenhouse' effect of global warming by $1°C–2°C$. This is enough to partly melt the polar ice caps and raise sea levels.

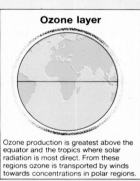

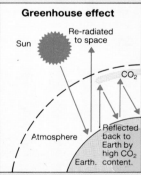

Figure E The ozone layer

species is now taking place on a large scale. Loss of species is particularly high in tropical forests, because deforestation is destroying many habitats. By the end of the century the world may be losing 50 000 species every year, or 130 each day.

QUESTIONS

1 a) What is meant by 'global warming'?
  b) Give TWO factors which may be contributing to global warming.
  c) How might global warming be affecting people?

2 Why are Norway and Sweden so concerned about the effects of acid rain? Are other countries also being affected?

3 Suppose there was a ban on the use of all aerosol sprays. In how many different wasy do you think this could affect your life?

Unit 11: Assessment

A World Environmental Conference

1 Look through this book again. Find examples of other world environmental problems which could have been included in this chapter. Write out a list of all of them
(10 marks)

2 Representatives of different groups of people concerned about the environment have been invited to a world environmental conference. Pupils should take on the role of representatives. The roles could include a:
   leader of a modern industrial country
   leader of a third world country
   grain farmer in North America
   peasant farmer in the Amazon Basin
   university lecturer in world climate
   university lecturer in geology
   head of a world wildlife organisation
   documentary film-maker
There should be enough roles for each person in the class.

3 Produce an agenda for the meeting. Do this by:
   a) making a 'short list' of the topics to be included. You will not have time to discuss all the topics you have thought of.
   b) listing them in order of priority for discussion.
(10 marks)
The agenda should be prepared and given out before the conference. Individuals or groups of representatives should prepare a topic for discussion and think about their views on the other topics.

4 At the conference each presentation should state the problem involved, its causes, and what should be done about it. The topic can then be discussed by others.
(20 marks)

5 After the conference prepare a poster or leaflet drawing the attention of the public to the main environmental problems.
(10 marks)
Total: 50 marks

UNITED NATIONS ENVIRONMENT PROGRAMME

Details of pupil profile sheet
Unit 11

Knowledge and understanding

1 Environmental hazards of living in Los Angeles
2 Major world environmental problems
3 Inter-relationships betwen these problems

Skills

1 Preparation of ideas and information for discussion
2 Contribution to class discussion in role-play
3 Production of poster or artwork

Values

1 Outlook of city dwellers in hazard-prone areas
2 Awareness of different views on major world environmental problems

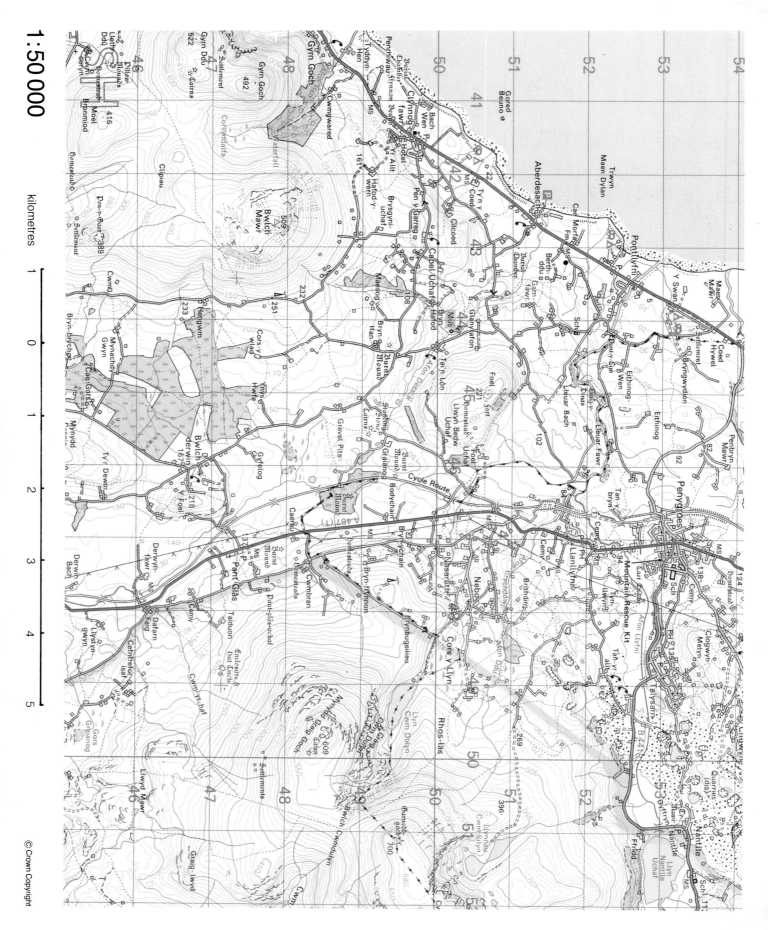

kilometres

1   0   1   2   3   4   5

Index

Pupil's Profile Sheet
Physical Environment and Human Activities

Unit ☐

Pupil name _____

After completing this unit you should be able to do the following

KNOWLEDGE AND UNDERSTANDING Understand and use the following terms and concepts:	YES	NO
1 _____		
2 _____		
3 _____		
4 _____		
5 _____		
6 _____		
7 _____		
8 _____		
9 _____		
10 _____		

SKILLS Understand and use the following skills:		
1 _____		
2 _____		
3 _____		
4 _____		
5 _____		
6 _____		
7 _____		
8 _____		
9 _____		
10 _____		

VALUES		
1 _____		
2 _____		
3 _____		